Liberalism And The Empire: Three Essays By Francis W. Hirst, Gilbert Murray And J. L. Hammond

Francis W. Hirst

Printing Statement:

Due to the very old age and scarcity of this book, many of the pages may be hard to read due to the blurring of the original text, possible missing pages, missing text, dark backgrounds and other issues beyond our control.

Because this is such an important and rare work, we believe it is best to reproduce this book regardless of its original condition.

Thank you for your understanding.

LIBERALISM AND THE EMPIRE

THREE ESSAYS

BY

FRANCIS W. HIRST   GILBERT MURRAY

AND

J. L. HAMMOND

LONDON
R. BRIMLEY JOHNSON
8 YORK BUILDINGS, ADELPHI
1900

DA
16
L43

All rights reserved

PREFACE

THE position of Great Britain as the Metropolis and centre of a world-wide nexus of free and prosperous commonwealths is one of the greatest features of contemporary history. It is a matter of just pride for Englishmen to reflect upon. It is a fundamental condition never to be lost sight of in any attempt at sound political thinking.

Our colonies, like most other colonies, owe their original existence, in one sense or another, to mere adventure or the power of the sword. They owe their vitality and strength, and most of the finer characteristics which make them almost unique in the history of colonization, to very different causes: to the policy of non-interference, to the studied avoidance of aggression, to toleration and generous amity between conflicting creeds and diverse races, to Liberal principles and Liberal ideas.

It has seemed to the writers of these Essays that there is at present grave danger of these higher con-

PREFACE

siderations being almost forgotten, and of force and aggression becoming not only too often employed as means towards good or tolerable ends, but actually worshipped and glorified as ends in themselves.

Authority, force, firmness, the detection of offences, the assertion of rightful claims and the punishment of enemies, are, no doubt, principles of great power and value in the world as it now stands; but they are not, and never have been, sufficient alone. Self-criticism, persuasion, patience, a wise blindness to offences, a reluctance to stand on the outermost edge of every right, the appeasement of enmities, are principles also of great and, one used to hope, of increasing value. On practical questions of politics the difference between the two English parties has generally been about the degree in which the first or authoritarian principles should be tempered or even supplanted by the second.

This difference of spirit has seldom come out more clearly than in the great speeches on the Parnell Commission. The Attorney-General collected elaborately every mischievous speech, every discreditable and criminal act committed by Irish Nationalists during a whole generation. He produced a most impressive catalogue, seethed with virtuous indignation, and called aloud for the punishment of so wicked a race. Sir Charles Russell, taking all the same facts, pointed out that agrarian crime generally follows agricultural distress, was in that instance increased by landlord

PREFACE

oppression and official misgovernment, and could only be diminished by reform. 'What! make concessions to criminals?' cried the Coercionists in anger. 'Forego our just revenge? Omit to assert our authority?' 'Certainly, if that will make things better,' is the Liberal reply.

What can be the feelings of so able and influential a Liberal as the Editor of the *Daily News* when he sees most English newspapers, and his own among them, filled day after day with statements, no doubt more or less well tested, intended to discredit, by hook or by crook, the whole race of South African Dutch, from reports of individual cruelties to natives, and explanations from adventurous financiers that their deficits are entirely due to bribes paid to the Volksraad, down to third-hand repetitions of what somebody told somebody that Mr. Reitz's brother had said eighteen years ago in a smoking-room? Must he not recognise that this is what we used to call 'Pigottism and Crime'; that it is like a certain newspaper's catalogues day by day of the crimes and abominations committed by members of the French army; like the old-fashioned attacks (now revived by the *National Review*) on the Jesuits; like the anti-Semite ravings against the Jews? Every sensible man knows that the French army, being very large and consisting of human beings, will produce a good daily crop of abominable actions, just as London without being in a blaze has three and a fraction houses on

PREFACE

fire every night. Every sensible man knows also that certain large bodies of men, such as Jews or Jesuits, will have certain tendencies as a class which other classes probably find objectionable. But every Liberal man, unless he be taken off his guard, will surely, above all things, resent a spirit of raking up evil which approaches so close to the mere spirit of slander; he will surely refuse to be drawn into hating whole multitudes of his fellow-creatures, into believing that Dutchmen are inherently so very different from Englishmen, or corruptible Hollanders so immeasurably worse than corrupting Rhodesians.

In South Africa the situation was one which cried aloud for Liberal and patient statesmanship. Two British colonies, one with a preponderatingly Dutch population; two autonomous Dutch States; ideas of federation in the air. It stood to reason that the right policy for Great Britain was conciliation and the obliteration of race differences. It was certain that racial feelings would exist. It was perfectly certain to anyone who knew the colonies that ambitious Dutchmen in the Transvaal would dream of a federated South Africa independent of the British flag; that ambitious English loyalists would wish to annex the two Dutch States, and to subordinate the Dutch to the British. 'Then war was inevitable!' says the Imperialist. Not at all; but war was dangerously possible. It was a statesman's business to see that these ambitious persons did not get the

PREFACE

upper hand, that these perilous dreams were not allowed to influence public policy.

As a matter of fact, they have dictated public policy. Mr. Rhodes's admirers admit him to be one of the most ambitious and unscrupulous of political financiers. The ascendancy of Mr. Rhodes in the councils of the English necessarily preserved the ascendancy of President Kruger among the Dutch. The extremist was met by the extremist, plotting by suspicion, and threats of violence by secret armaments. Conspirators, backed by a Prime Minister, invaded the Transvaal in time of peace, and tried to assassinate the Boers in their sleep. The Boers chanced to be awake, and the plot failed. The invaders were beaten, made prisoners, spared by President Kruger, and handed over for trial to the British Government. The Prime Minister of the Cape was proved to be the chief criminal: he was not punished, not even removed from the list of Her Majesty's secret counsellors. The chief organ of the Government, when found in the thick of the plot, and detected—as by other Royal Commissions—in publishing false documents, escaped scot-free. The guilty complicity of the Colonial Secretary was, and is, gravely suspected even in England and Scotland, generally believed in Ireland, and accepted as obvious in the two Dutch States and in most of the Foreign Offices of Europe.

Yes, if that was to be England's policy and these

PREFACE

her standards of international honour, if, lastly, the same spirit and the same men that produced and screened the Jameson Raid were to remain constitutionally in power in England and surreptitiously in power at the Cape, then, indeed, the war was inevitable. To avoid it would have needed wisdom, generosity, patience, statesmanship. And where was 'Imperialist' England to find such things?

All the last three wars so lightly undertaken would have been avoided by Liberal statesmanship. In India we should have acted according to Lord Curzon's later thoughts and not according to his first thoughts; we should not have committed the 'breach of faith.' We should not have had the almost motiveless expedition to the Soudan, with its barren and intoxicating splendour; its necessary weakening of our military power by the locking up of British and Egyptian soldiers to hold a remote desert; its Oriental pageant of revenges, extended, it is to be feared, even to the wounded, and in one case to the dead.

The Afridi War was successful, the Soudan War brilliantly triumphant. The South African War is, from the military point of view, unsatisfactory; from the political point of view, disastrous. In a year or two, no doubt, ordinary politicians will be anxious to condemn the South African War. But true Liberals will reject all responsibility for the successful wars as well as for the unsuccessful, not because they

PREFACE

were wars—some wars have been necessary and even glorious—but because they were unjust and uncalled-for wars, the products of crude, boyish ambitions and unworthy policy.

A fabric of human lives so vast as that for which Her Majesty's Government is now responsible surely demands for its good guidance both high principles and profound prudence. Does the ordinary educated man, either Liberal or Conservative, who reads the *Times* and studies Mr. Chamberlain's speeches, find in them either such prudence or such principles? Apart from the indiscretions of the Colonial Secretary's diplomacy, apart from the deplorable tendency of the great newspaper to organize crusades—and very sinister and rash crusades—instead of publishing facts, we believe it will scarcely be disputed that the ordinary good citizen recognises in both these guides of modern England a standard of conduct and a code of honour markedly inferior to his own. If so, why does he tolerate and follow them? Is it perhaps the same spirit which sometimes leads a personally upright man to be rather pleased than otherwise at the sharp practice of his own lawyer? 'The solicitor's honour is his own concern; we need not grumble, provided he will win us our case.' It may be with some such feelings that many people are inclined to regard the *Times* and Mr. Chamberlain as lawyers for England. They can be trusted never to understate their clients' claims; and if they over-

PREFACE

state them, if they do sometimes twist awkward facts and intimidate honest witnesses, it is not for us to be squeamish; the other party can find that out! Such reasoning is no more wise than it is honourable. We are beginning already to see the fruits of it in the general increase of navies, the hatred of England among civilized peoples, the suspicion of England among civilized Governments. A power which has alienated the goodwill of mankind is in a more precarious position than a power with too small an army, and few kings or nations have lived long after accepting for their rule of life the inhuman principle, *Oderint dum metuant.*

There is no sentiment in a nation so dangerous, there is no sentiment so easy to stimulate, as the false excess of patriotism. There is probably no country in the world from China to Peru in which the sub-conscious voices of national egotism do not persistently whisper in men's ears the same intoxicating tale: '"We are the pick and flower of nations, and (in one sense or another) the chosen people of God! Various foreigners may or may not have their good points, but only we are really whole and right and normal. Other nations boast and are aggressive; only we are modest and content with our barest due, though it is obvious that we are by nature specially qualified for ruling others, and no unprejudiced person can doubt that our present territories ought to be increased. That our yoke is a pure

PREFACE

blessing to all who come under it is a plain fact, proved by the almost unanimous testimony of our own citizens, our historians, our missionaries, our soldiers, our travellers, and only denied out of spite by a few envious foreigners, whom no one believes!"'

Sentiments like these — call them patriotism, Jingoism, Chauvinism, or what you will—form a strong and persistent force, valuable when checked, dangerous when stimulated, and charged with all the elements of exasperation and explosion whenever there is most need for patience and for care.

There is also in most civilized countries another party, inspired, consciously or unconsciously, by the older school of English Liberals, who do not accept the extravagant pretensions of their own countrymen; who judge of national honour by more or less the same standards as they apply to private honour; who believe in international morality and in the co-operation of nations for mutual help; who, if they are to dream at all, will dream not of Armageddons and Empires, but of progress and freedom, and the ultimate fraternity of mankind.

If the Chauvinist and Jingo parties become predominant in the various nations of Europe, security and progress will become constantly more difficult, commerce will decline, our manufacturing supremacy will disappear, and 'inevitable' wars, with their inevitable accompaniments of suffering and poverty, will become the staple food of politics. And each

PREFACE

aggressive step taken by the Jingoes of one nation is a stimulus to the Jingoes of every other.

We are threatened at this moment with a 'khaki' General Election. Military politicians and political soldiers were agreeing not long ago that the time was 'not unpropitious' for a war with France. Popular newspapers and preachers were vying with one another in collecting the most damaging facts, in spreading broadcast the most subtle slanders, against the most Liberal of Continental nations; in sowing hatred and mutual distrust between the two great pioneer peoples of humanity and enlightenment. Is there not here a danger against which all liberal and humane men, all moderate men, all sensible men, should unite their forces? France has shown her self-restraint. She is trying to suppress her own mischief-makers; let us respond to her by at least curbing ours.

A true statesman will learn from his neighbours and help his neighbours. He will not waste his strength on hating and dreading his neighbours. He will not turn aside from the management of a vast and most imperfect State to cut the throats of Dervishes and Dutchmen, and speculate on the best ways of injuring Germany and Russia. In England, Heaven knows, there is enough widespread suffering to remedy, enough rampant injustice to redress, enough preventable crime unprevented, enough avenues of social improvement to lay open and

PREFACE

develop. There is enough work to be done in fostering the unity and reality of the free British commonwealths, in razing our own fortresses of monopoly and privilege, in intervening on behalf of oppressed and deluded citizens in our own country, in gathering fresh material for wise legislation from those vast stores of political experience and matured sagacity in which England surpasses all nations.

We need not spend the greatest proportion of our time and energy and treasure on plans for increasing our territories and dreams of proving by sword and fire the superiority and divine mission of the Anglo-Saxon race; there are better ways to prove them.

The writers of these three essays are not 'Little Englanders,' nor are they for 'peace at any price.' They are alive to the need of adequate defences. They are blind neither to the glories nor yet to the responsibilities of the British Empire. They may regret the common use of that word as ambiguous and unfortunate. 'Empire' is the rule of one nation over other nations. We hold empire over India, over the Soudan; we do not hold empire over Canada or Australia. Free Canada and free Australia are grander evidences of England's greatness and solider elements in her strength than all those tropical provinces which she has won as a conqueror and holds as a foreign despot.

The word 'empire' has blurred this great distinction. More, it has infected ordinary English thought

PREFACE

about the colonies with associations drawn from the regions that are ruled despotically and held by the sword. Even so laudable a movement as that for the federation of all the free English commonwealths began by calling itself 'Imperial,' and ended by pinning its whole faith to militarism and protection and certain large financial enterprises!

The greatness of Greater Britain lies not in these things, and is not compatible with these things. Our conceptions of it must be utterly freed from the false atmosphere that has now clogged and blinded them. The present writers believe that for many years past the aggressive and vainglorious instincts of Great Britain have been unduly stimulated; that adventure, conquest, mastery, and race-pride, strangely wedded with speculative finance and culminating in the fatal lust of Empire, have been so long held up to the worship of the populace by men whose position and antecedents should have rendered them capable of higher, or at least of saner, ideals, that the reason of the country is in abeyance and its imagination intoxicated, and possibilities are brought near to us which may involve in vital danger even a commonwealth so massively stable as our own. In this belief they have ventured to raise their voices.

The three essays which constitute this book are all alike animated by the principles laid down in this Preface, though of course each writer is responsible

PREFACE

only for his own statements. The first paper is an attempt to explore the finance of imperialism, and to show how militarism and excessive expenditure upon armaments both feed and are fed by calculated panics and 'inevitable wars,' which serve at the same time another purpose — that of preventing reforms at home. The second seeks by the help of a historical parallel to analyze one part of the relation of Great Britain to her subject races; and, while making only the most tentative proposals of reform, endeavours at least to call attention to the dire gravity of the problem. In the third and last a contrast is drawn between the leading ideas of Liberalism in foreign policy and the teaching of modern imperialism; the morality, the tendencies and the fruits of imperialism are discussed, and an attempt is made to show that the desertion of our great traditions is inconsistent with the greatness and the safety of the Empire.

CONTENTS

IMPERIALISM AND FINANCE

By Francis W. Hirst

I

EFFICIENCY and economy, 1-3; rise of Imperialism, 3, 4; growth of armaments, 5-7; Mr. Cobden and the Three Panics, 7-16; Mr. Gladstone's financial policy in the sixties, 17-20; Lord Palmerston and Mr. Chamberlain, 20, 21; contrast of Gladstonian and Unionist finance, 21-25; the Fourth Panic and the navy, 26-28; Mr. Goschen and aggressive expenditure, 28-32; its effects abroad and at home, 32-34; recent outlay on the army and the views of Sir M. Hicks-Beach, 35-41.

II

Financial Imperialism and war, 41-45; Rhodesianism and Mr. Rhodes, 45-47; the De Beers monopoly, 47-49; the Chartered Company, 50-55; the financiers and the South African War, 56-59; the Raid, Mr. Rhodes, and Mr. Chamberlain, 60-62; the manipulation of the press, 62-66; Emporialism, Free Trade, and war for commerce, 67-75.

CONTENTS

III

Municipal finance and the growth of rates, 76-79; the principles of our law of rating, 80-82; absurdity of the present system, 82-85; why and how urban land should be rated, 86-94; the license duties, and alcoholic liquor as a fiscal monopoly, 95-101.

IV

The relations between local and imperial finance, 102; the Budgets of 1899 and 1900, 102, 103; attack by the *Times* upon Free Trade, 104-110; Protection and militarism, 110-112; the rule of the rich and its remedies, including Payment of Members, 113-115; dividends in politics, and Africa in England, 115-117.

THE EXPLOITATION OF INFERIOR RACES IN ANCIENT AND MODERN TIMES

By Gilbert Murray

An Imperial labour question, with a historical parallel

An Imperial labour problem, 118; division of labour among races, 119-121; this principle essential in ancient slavery, the slave being an alien, 121, 122; general consideration of the employment of captive or destitute aliens in ancient communities, 122, 123; development of slavery in Greece, intimately connected with colonization, and based on economic causes, 124, 125; the case of Athens, 126-129; of Rome, 129-131; ancient criticism of slavery, 131-134: modern analogies: full slavery, 134; corvée, 135; exportation of the alien under indenture, 136; Chinese labour, 137; other cheap alien labour: Polish, Irish, negro, Italian, 138-140; em-

CONTENTS

ployment of the alien in his own country, characteristically modern, 140, 141 ; South African systems, 141, 142 ; compounds and locations, 143-145 ; aliens as soldiers, 145 ; re-statement of the problem : the essence of slavery, 147-150 ; the future, 150, 151 ; cruelties involved in juxtaposition of higher and lower races, 152-154 ; possible alleviations, 154-157.

COLONIAL AND FOREIGN POLICY

BY J. L. HAMMOND

Comparison of present position with political conditions in Fox's time, 158, 159 ; disposition to suppose that Liberal Party can only escape annihilation by accepting Imperialism, 160 ; an effect of the fashionable fatalism, 161 ; that fatalism unscientific and demoralizing, 162 ; foreign to the spirit which made Liberal foreign policy, 163 ; what that Liberalism did, 164 ; Mr. Gladstone's Liberalism : (1) morality, 165 ; (2) nationalism, 166 ; England an inheritor and guardian of European civilization, 167-170 ; Imperialism stands for the very opposite ideas, 170 ; morality, 171, 172 ; a pseudo-scientific confusion, 172, 173 ; the Imperalist argument from civilization, 174, 175 ; Mr. Gladstone on 'imperium et libertas,' 177 ; our unpopularity abroad, 178, 179 ; some effects of the new morality, 180-184 ; Imperialism and Nationalism, 155-190; the influence of the internationals, 191, 192 ; diplomacy of last few years lacking in continuity, 193 196 ; Imperialism and peace, 196 ; Imperialism and Anglo-French relations, 198, 199 ; Mr. Gladstone and Imperialism, 200-206 ; Liberalism and Ireland, India, the Colonies, 207-209 ; Liberalism in foreign relations the condition of domestic progress, 210.

LIBERALISM AND THE EMPIRE

An uneasy smile flits over the faces of the initiated: another public imposture is publicly renounced:
'Solvuntur risu tabulæ.'

The old metal has been thrown into the melting-pot, and poured back into a new mould, to take the types of a new diplomacy, a new finance, and a new statesmanship. The people stand by passive, unconsulted, uninstructed, puzzled, doubtful; they are halting between two centuries and two opinions.

The writer of the following pages does not pretend to have any secrets to impart or any mysteries to divulge. He well knows that the river of prodigality may be traced to a perennial spring. But experience, which tells us that the stream of profusion and corruption will always run, tells us also by what arts its volume may be swollen into a furious and devastating flood, and by what management it may be regulated and reduced to a harmless rivulet.

A democracy is reasonable as well as changeable; it is open to intellectual and, still more, to moral conviction; it is idealist rather than materialist; it will take bribes, but it prefers doctrines. The political character, as seen in the political history, of Great Britain is the answer to the false prophets who warn us not to battle for the impossible, to adjust our inclinations to what cannot be helped, to bow down and worship the doctrine of the inevitable. Belief in the people, a confident anticipation that they will judge rightly if only the truth can be put before them, is at once the justification and the consolation of the scattered garrisons who have kept the Liberal flag flying amid the surrenders and the desertions of the last few months.

'I know,' said Burke (in proposing an unpopular reform which had only 'the cold commendation of public advantage ')—'I know it is common for men to say that such and such things are perfectly right —very desirable ; but that, unfortunately, they are not practicable. Oh no, sir — no. Those things which are not practicable are not desirable. There is nothing in the world really beneficial that does not lie within the reach of an informed understanding and a well-directed pursuit. There is nothing that God has judged good for us that He has not given us the means to accomplish, both in the natural and the moral world.'

At the present time the body politic is suffering from many evil humours; some have arisen naturally, some have been artificially produced. None can be cured except by the sanguine and defiant spirit of the reformer, and for none is that spirit needed in such ample measure as for that which stands out as the giant upas-tree of our time, for beside it all other evils are secondary; they multiply beneath its shadow and grow under its protection.

The poisonous growth of Imperialism was scorched (as it seemed, utterly blasted and consumed) by Mr. Gladstone in 1879-80; but new seedlings sprang

LIBERALISM AND THE EMPIRE

up, and flourished in what he called at one mournful crisis his 'political decrepitude.' One of these (which has grown to the greatest height) shows certain peculiarities that seem to justify it in applying to be enrolled as a new species of the genus Imperialism. The first species was the bluff military imperialism of Lord Palmerston. Then shot up the sham imperialism of Lord Beaconsfield. The third and most poisonous species grows in auriferous soil; it is the financial or speculative imperialism of Mr. Rhodes,[1] and is much cultivated by enterprising colonists from Syrophœnicia. What, then, is imperialism? What is this giant upas-tree that has to be cut down? What are the poisons which it exhales? what are its main branches? Do its roots strike deep? What is the character of the earth in which it takes root and flourishes?

In the painful recovery from economic exhaustion following the Napoleonic wars, Liberal doctrines began to spread slowly through English society, and at last pierced here and there the intellectual gloom that had settled over the governing classes when Pitt sold his soul and his country to the war party, Continental despotism, and the Court.

---

[1] Some think that Mr. Chamberlain has raised a separate variety, dependent upon a supposed connection between Trade and the Flag, and a confusion between *emporium* and *imperium*. Of which later. Perhaps it may be called, provisionally, 'Emporialism.'

IMPERIALISM AND FINANCE

From 1815 up to 1832 a reduction of armaments was dictated mainly by the poverty of the people, and the fear of rulers that economic discontent might breed revolution. After the passing of the Reform Bill, the principles of public economy and of common-sense made way so rapidly that the imperialism and militarism of that time took alarm, and set out in the press and in Parliament to work up middle-class panics in the interests of the services; and particularly of the navy—for it was hopeless to try to persuade our grandfathers that a big army was necessary for security. The normal ratio of the English to the French navy was at that time as three to two, and our expenditure upon this arm was raised from £4,245,000 in 1835 to £5,824,000 in 1840. The drain emptied our Treasury and injured our credit. France followed suit; and when, in 1841, the country, disgusted with the Whigs, returned Sir Robert Peel at the head of an immense Conservative majority, the proportions between the English and French navy had altered unfavourably to our own country. Peel, who was preparing the first great instalment of Free Trade, and making the first serious effort to reduce the National Debt, declared in the House of Commons, without loss of time, his conviction, as First Minister of the Crown, that 'the true interest of Europe is to come to some one common accord, so as to enable every country to reduce those military armaments which belong to a state of war rather than of peace'; and he expressed an earnest wish 'that the Councils of every country (or that the public voice and mind if the Councils did not) would willingly propagate such a doctrine.'

The expenditure of Great Britain upon her army and navy provided for in the estimates of that year (1841) was £13,392,000. Sir Robert Peel asked whether the time had not come to declare that 'there is no use in such overgrown establishments.'

'What is the advantage of one Power greatly increasing its army and navy? Does it not see that other Powers will follow its example? The consequences of this must be that no increase of relative strength will accrue to any one Power; but there must be a universal consumption of the resources of every country in military preparations.'

In the spring of 1899 the estimates of Lord Salisbury's Government for military and naval expenditure for the ensuing year amounted to $49\frac{1}{2}$ millions of money. A corresponding increase had taken place in the size and cost of Continental armaments. This time, not the Prime Minister of Great Britain, but the Czar of All the Russias took the initiative. A Conference was summoned at the Hague. Our representatives insisted on excluding the Transvaal Republic, and stood out for the use of the Dum-dum bullet. The attitude of our Ministry might be gathered from the sneers of their supporters in the

IMPERIALISM AND FINANCE

press and in Parliament, or from the militant, arrogant, and offensive language of certain of its members. Our prophets and scribes had come to think that peace would not 'pay.'

The policy outlined by Sir Robert Peel, and imperfectly realized by the Peelites, Cobdenites, and philosophical Radicals in the twelve years preceding the Crimean War, and again by the united Liberal party under Mr. Gladstone in the interval (say, 1863-76) between the collapse of the third panic and the development of Disraelite imperialism, was the policy formulated by Mr. Cobden's political genius, and illuminated by the splendid eloquence of Mr. Bright. We may doubt whether there is any example in the annals of popular government of a practical wisdom so perseveringly and so successfully applied to contemporary evils. Though the gap created by Mr. Cobden's death could not be filled, his disciples were long able to maintain the ground won by him. Scarcely a whisper of Protection was heard for thirty years after his death; militarism drooped and hung its head; the spirit of aggressive imperialism only once struggled into predominance.

In *The Three Panics* (perhaps the most brilliant and convincing piece from even that political pen) Mr. Cobden teaches lessons which should be laid to heart by the degenerate England of to-day. The first panic, of 1845-48, had its pretext in some naval projects (rather than preparations) made by France in consequence of the Syrian dispute. There were unscrupulous politicians on this side of the Channel who interested themselves in keeping alive the feeling of irritation—lineal ancestors of those who love to harp upon the incident of Fashoda—and it seemed as though the French Government 'sought to console the nation for the wounds which had been inflicted on its self-love by enormous and costly preparations for future wars.'[1] In the year 1848 the bogey of a French invasion was suddenly thrust upon the public.

The Duke of Wellington, then Commander-in-Chief, in his seventy-seventh year, wrote that on the whole coast from the North Foreland to Selsey Bill 'there is not a spot on which infantry might not be thrown on shore at any time of tide, with any wind, and in any weather.' Lord Palmerston, who could not plead dotage, almost outdid the Duke's delusion in the speeches which fanned the second panic (1852); for he declared that, steam navigation having bridged the Channel, fifty or sixty thousand men could be transported without notice or warning from Cherbourg to our shores in a single night; or if not absolutely without notice, certainly 'without our having lengthened or, indeed, even timely notice.'

There were one or two fairly intelligent 'Service members' in the House who could not swallow this. But Lord Palmerston was not to be denied:

[1] Cobden's Political Writings, 1868 edition, vol. ii., p. 224.

IMPERIALISM AND FINANCE

'The very ship despatched to convey to this country intelligence of the threatened armament would probably not reach our shores much sooner than the hostile expedition.'

The first invasion panic was killed partly by the proposal of the Ministry to add 5d. in the £ to the income-tax, and partly by the arrival in England of the dread monarch, Louis Philippe, not as an invader but as a fugitive.

'Public meetings were called, men of influence, of different political parties, mingled on the same platform to denounce the increase of taxation, to repudiate the desire for the militia, or any other addition to the defensive armaments of the country, and to call for a reduction of the public expenditure.'[1]

So great is the pacifying effect of fivepence.

'Hi motus animorum, atque hæc certamina tanta,
Pulveris exigui jactu compressa quiescunt.'

The panic-mongers did their best with the hideous apparition of a new Republic, but they could accomplish nothing. To the dismay of the services, and the great benefit of the taxpayers, successive reductions of the military and naval expenditure were effected between 1847 and 1851. But the country, thanks to Free Trade and the discoveries of gold, was advancing 'towards that state of prosperity in which

---

[1] Cobden's Political Works, 1868 edition, vol. ii., p. 233.

its timidity and pugnacity seem equally susceptible of excitement.' The *coup d'état* of December, 1851, was the signal for a fresh outbreak in the metropolitan journals and a fresh eruption of pamphlets.

Ministers, after protesting against the inflammatory violence of the Yellow Press,[1] themselves succumbed and intimated that they would prepare against an impossible invasion. Lord John Russell prepared a Militia Bill, but resigned when Lord Palmerston's amendment (extending its scope) was carried.

Lord Derby then became Lord Palmerston's instrument, and a Bill was passed into law authorizing the creation of a militia force, and involving the country in a large expenditure to guard against an imaginary danger.

Thus an increase of the army was brought about by a panic artificially created and utterly devoid of basis. It was due, said old Joseph Hume, not like bygone panics, to the old women, 'but to our having too many clubs about London containing too many half-pay officers who had nothing to do but look after themselves and their friends. These were the people who wrote to the newspapers,

---

[1] Their protest, as well as their practice, was supported by a patriotic Opposition : 'I say that it is more than imprudent, that it is more than injudicious, that it is more than folly—that it is perfect madness.'—Lord Derby, speaking of the attacks on France and the French President in the debate on the Address, 1852.

IMPERIALISM AND FINANCE

anxious to bring grist to the mill somehow or other.' A naval member added jocularly 'that the alarm about invasion was chiefly expressed by soldiers, from the illustrious Duke downwards.' Army men could not or would not comprehend the difficulties of transporting soldiers or of landing them in the face of a superior fleet. However, the navy had its turn. The Naval Secretary adopted a mysterious style of panic oratory which would have done credit to Mr. Goschen; and the Opposition Front Bench abandoned its functions of criticism and accepted the doctrine of 'abject confidence in the Ministry.' Thus in a few months' time large additions were made to our military and naval establishments by Lord Derby and his Tory colleagues, who, as long as they were so engaged, met with support from their opponents; but, this mischievous task achieved, 'thenceforth the benefit of implicit confidence in the Executive was no longer extended to them, and a few days afterwards they were overthrown in a division on the Budget.'[1]

Lord Aberdeen's Ministry of All the Talents took office in 1852. But neither change of Ministry nor increase of armaments allayed the agitation. French plans for seizing London and sacking it, stories of French war-vessels hovering about Dover and the Isle of Wight, filled the newspapers; and every half-pay officer had a pamphlet out on the 'Invasion of

[1] Cobden's Political Writings, 1868 edition, vol. ii., p. 256.

LIBERALISM AND THE EMPIRE

England,' the 'Peril of Portsmouth,' or the 'Defensive Resources of Great Britain.'

Meanwhile France was engaged in the peaceful pursuits of economy. In February, 1853, the French Minister of Marine wrote to an English acquaintance that the warlike preparations ascribed to him by the English press were all purely fictitious. He had not armed a single gunboat or equipped a single sailor.

'I remain the calm spectator of the enormous expenses you are making to conjure away an imaginary danger; and I admire the facility with which you augment your Budget when no real necessity prescribes it.'

And in a letter to a colleague the same Minister alluded in a delightful vein of irony to the members of the English Cabinet 'who are covering themselves with armour, and who possibly may not be very much distressed by these imaginary terrors (as we have sometimes seen among ourselves), inasmuch as they enable them to swell their Budget and serve to strengthen a somewhat uncertain majority in Parliament.' In fact, the total French expenditure on the navy had fallen from £5,145,000 in 1847 to £3,462,000 in 1852. Unfortunately, the best-informed editors often collect their information and write their leaders not as men 'labouring up the hill of heavenly truth,' but with steps bent on another quest, down an easy incline towards a different place. The press monopoly, which helped in the spring and

IMPERIALISM AND FINANCE

summer of 1899, by the device of a Dutch conspiracy and the fabrication of Boer atrocities, to produce the popular feeling requisite to the designs of Mr. Rhodes, Mr. Chamberlain, and Sir Alfred Milner, was created by extraneous financial influences.[1] In 1852-53, however, 'a monopoly of publicity' was virtually possessed by the *Times*, 'whose conductors,' in the words of Mr. Cobden, 'had thus the power of giving the impress of public opinion to whatever views they chose to espouse.' Its columns 'teemed with the most violent denunciations of the French ruler, mixed with expressions of contempt for the people of France,' which were reproduced almost *totidem verbis* in September, 1899, only to give place to grateful flattery in the early months of 1900. One of its anonymous correspondents of the earlier period, 'An Englishman,' was betrayed into expressions not obscurely suggestive of assassination.

Violence, however, produced a reaction. An influential meeting of London merchants and bankers protested against the attempt to create ill-will and hostility between the two great nations. A deputation was sent to the French Emperor. The current of press-conducted jingoism was diverted into another channel. In a year's time Napoleon the tyrant, our best friend and ally, was drifted on the same rudderless craft with Lord Aberdeen and his helpless crew

[1] See Mr. Hobson's chapter on 'A Chartered Press,' in his 'War in South Africa,' 1900.

LIBERALISM AND THE EMPIRE

into the Black Sea of the Crimean War. '*Drifted!*' —the very word used by our Foreign Minister, Lord Clarendon, of the helpless diplomacy which resulted in that unnecessary and fruitless conflict. '*Drifted!*' —a fatalism, a past echo of the familiar doctrine of the inevitable. Mr. Cobden has described the state of the British people in the spring of 1853:

'The nation had grown rich and prosperous with a rapidity beyond all precedent. Our exports had risen from £52,849,000 in 1848 to £98,933,000 in 1853, having nearly doubled in five years.' As in 1899, so it happened in 1854. Fuel mischievously set alight for a small bonfire fed a mighty conflagration. 'History shows that such a condition of things is fruitful in national follies and crimes, of which war is but the greatest. The time is not yet, though it will come, when people will be able to bear the blessings of prosperity and liberty with peace.'[1]

Here we have the most reasonable formula which scientific imagination has developed from the political psychology of war. Elsewhere[2] the doctrine is elaborated:

'In ordinary years, when nothing occurs to concentrate public attention on this branch of the Budget, it will be observed that the expenditure on the services has a tendency to increase in proportion to the prosperity

[1] Cobden's Political Writings, 1868 edition, vol. ii., p. 268.
[2] *Ibid.*, p. 235.

of the country. Taking the amount of our foreign trade as the test of the progress of the nation, we shall find, looking back over the last ten or twelve years, that the amount of the exports and the amount of military and naval estimates have been augmented in a nearly equal ratio, both having been about doubled. It would seem as if there were some unseen power behind the Government, always able, *unless held in check by an agitation in the country*, to help itself to a portion of the national savings, limited only by the taxable patience of the public.'

If to the words italicized 'or by determined Ministers' be added, this will be found to be a substantially accurate statement,[1] arrived at empirically by an examination of our financial history from 1832 to 1862, and empirically confirmed by a further examination of that history from 1862 to 1900. To put Mr. Cobden's formula to the test is not foreign to our purpose, especially as much historical comfort may be derived by those who believe in trying to counteract bad tendencies even when they are called 'popular movements' or 'the march of democratic progress.' Take by way of illustration the years 1859-66. During the whole of that period Mr. Gladstone was

---

[1] Mr. Cobden's suggestion of a ratio between the variations in the values of exports and the cost of military and naval establishments must not, of course, be pressed. It is only a tendency—what a nation would do if it were ordinarily foolish and easy-going.

LIBERALISM AND THE EMPIRE

Chancellor of the Exchequer. The first three of these years cover the third of the three panics. The incidents of the panic and of the military expenditure which it enabled its chief promoter, Lord Palmerston, to force upon his unwilling Chancellor of the Exchequer, and especially the strange contrast between the commercial treaty with the French Emperor and the fortification scheme against him, are inimitably depicted by Mr. Cobden. Setting one thing against another, we must own that Lord Palmerston and his lieutenants, the Duke of Somerset and Mr. Sidney Herbert, drew away from Mr. Gladstone at the start. Yet, taking Mr. Cobden's criterion of prosperity, the wind was against them. The total value of our exports, which stood at 130 millions in 1859, and at 136 millions in 1860, sank to 125 and 124 millions respectively in the two following years. But look at the military expenditure.

	ARMY.	NAVY.
Expenditure for the year ending March 31, 1859	£ 12,512,000	£ 9,215,000
Expenditure for the year ending March 31, 1860	14,057,000	11,823,000
Expenditure for the year ending March 31, 1861	14,970,000	13,331,000
Expenditure for the year ending March 31, 1862	15,570,000	12,598,000
Expenditure for the year ending March 31, 1863	16,254,000	11,370,000

IMPERIALISM AND FINANCE

The real increase in the expenditure upon the navy is greater by about a million than that exhibited in the table, because the cost of the Post Office Packet Service, which was included in the first two years, is excluded in the last three—an improved system of accounts having been adopted. There must also be added the cost of the fortification scheme, for which power was taken in the Budget of 1860-61 to raise £9,000,000. I think about £3,000,000 was spent in that way in the years 1861-62-63.

Mr. Gladstone's great Free Trade Budget of 1860, embodying the tariff reductions necessitated by the French Commercial Treaty, has always been compared with his earlier and equally famous Budget of 1853. In each case Mr. Gladstone made large remissions of Customs Duties; nor did the two sets of remissions differ substantially in character. But there was a remarkable contrast in the results. In 1853-54 Customs Duties to the amount of £1,500,000 were remitted, and the loss was more than made up within the year. In 1860-61 the Chancellor of the Exchequer took off £2,376,000 in duties; but he only recovered £580,000. Similar changes in the Excise Duties exhibited a still more remarkable contrast. In his Budget speech (April 15th, 1861) Mr. Gladstone could only account for the comparative want of elasticity shown in the revenue of the previous year, as compared with that of 1853-54, by the difference in national expenditure. In seven years our imperial (*i.e.*, non-local) expenditure had mounted from 56 to 73 millions. Mr. Gladstone could not help 'suspecting that there may be some degree of relation between the inordinate growth of expenditure and the diminished elasticity of the revenue.' He computed that the total savings of the nation[1] for the past eight years had been 'completely absorbed and swallowed up in the maw of the vast expenditure.'

The total value of exports, which had sunk, as we saw, to 124 millions in 1862, now began to rise rapidly. It stood at 147 millions in 1863, 160 millions in 1864, and 166 millions in 1865. In 1866 it amounted to no less than 189 millions. Here was an increase in British exports of more than 50 per cent.; and a normal increase of about the same proportions was 'inevitable' in our military and naval estimates. But the inevitable was not allowed to happen. A Minister with a strong will and with good support in the country and in the House of Commons was labouring in the interests of public economy against the craze for armaments.

The gross expenditure of the country, which had stood at £72,792,000 in 1860-61, had been brought

[1] The interest, that is to say, on the amount which 'the skill and the capital and the industry and the thrift' of the country might be computed to have laid by in those eight years.

IMPERIALISM AND FINANCE

down as low as £65,914,000 in 1865-66. It would be hard to exaggerate the commercial benefits which Mr. Gladstone's financial policy heaped upon the nation during these years. The income-tax was reduced from tenpence to fourpence. The duties upon hundreds of articles, manufactured and unmanufactured, from silks, woollens, linens, leather, and artificial flowers, to eggs, cheese, butter, paper, and dates, were swept away, and enormous reductions were effected in the duties upon timber, tea, sugar, and other important commodities.

The following table shows the downward movement of military expenditure:

	Army.	Navy.
	£	£
Expenditure for the year ending March 31, 1864	14,638,000	10,821,000
Expenditure for the year ending March 31, 1865	14,382,000	10,898,000
Expenditure for the year ending March 31, 1866	13,804,000	10,259,000

Considerable as were the natural surpluses in some of these years, they would readily have been absorbed by the military and naval services if the Exchequer had been in the charge of a weak and yielding Chancellor. They were in a great degree created by wise economy and by the steady application of the maxim not then dishonoured or disused, 'Magnum vectigal est parsimonia.' Nor would it be claimed by Sir Michael Hicks-Beach

LIBERALISM AND THE EMPIRE

(on whose policy in a period of even greater natural prosperity it will be needful to concentrate attention) that Mr. Gladstone had no pressure to contend against. He had a Prime Minister who personified military imperialism and a 'spirited' foreign policy. To a Palmerston, Lord Salisbury would have seemed a peace-at-any-price-man. There was also in the Ministry a Secretary for War who 'wanted to see'—so he once assured the House of Commons—'a military spirit pervading all classes of the community; but especially the influential and intelligent great middle class.'[1] With, perhaps, a dozen notorious exceptions, the Liberal Opposition in the Commons and the Lords has not contributed to panic measures and the growth of armaments since 1895. It was otherwise with the Opposition in 1859 and the early sixties. Liberal Imperialists like Mr. Horsman[2] and independent Tories like Lord Lyndhurst were more eloquent and not less panic-stricken than the Mr. Perks and Lord Wemyss of

[1] On May 9th, 1900, the Primrose League was exhorted by Lord Glenesk to co-operate with Her Majesty's Ministers ' in furthering the military spirit which is so prominent in our midst.' We must wake up, he cried, to the fact that 'we want each Englishman to be a self-contained warrior in himself.'

[2] On July 23rd, 1860, Mr. Horsman listened with 'satisfaction' to a speech of Lord Palmerston, which he declared to have been 'one of the most serious and alarming speeches he had ever heard delivered by a Minister of the Crown in time of peace.'

our own day. Mr. Chamberlain himself with his 'long spoon,' his 'mend your manners,' his 'squeezed sponge,' and his 'hour-glass,' could not have been a more inconvenient colleague than the author of the following declaration—which was intended, of course, for French consumption:

'We accept with frankness the right hand of friendship wherever it is tendered to us. We do not distrust that proffered right hand because we see the left hand grasping the hilt of the sword. But when that left hand plainly does so grasp the hilt of the sword it would be extreme folly in us to throw away our shield of defence.'[1] The God of Panics is ally and precursor of the God of Battles.

Mr. Gladstone's first and greatest Ministry (1868-74) was also equal to the task of preventing the inevitable, and of securing to the country not only peace, influence, and comity in foreign relations, but retrenchments and reform at home. Diplomacy and arbitration took the place of war; we were not betrayed by wild-cat theories of defence into aggressive armaments. Prosperity went to reduce taxation instead of inflating the estimates. The average annual expenditure upon the navy in the five years during which Mr. Gladstone's Government held office was between nine and ten millions. The cost of the army, which Mr. Disraeli had increased to nearly $15\frac{1}{2}$ millions in 1868, was reduced in the five years

[1] Lord Palmerston at Dover, August 28th, 1861.

LIBERALISM AND THE EMPIRE

following to an average of about 13¾ millions. But there was no suggestion (so far as I am aware) made from any authoritative quarter at the General Election of 1874 that the Services had not maintained their reputation. Nay, Mr. Cardwell's army reforms stand out with solitary splendour in the dismal records of War Office organization. If the navy was starved, it continued to be starved all through the seventies. In 1874 the total value of British exports had risen to 297 millions sterling, the National Debt had been considerably reduced, the emancipation of industry by Free Trade Legislation was accomplished, and Mr. Gladstone was in a position to offer to the country the abolition of the income-tax.

The next period of commercial prosperity and elastic revenues at all comparable to those already passed in review will probably reach its climax in the present financial year, if it has not already done so in the year ended March 31st, 1900. The 1859-66 series and the 1868-74 series began with war and the growth of armaments, and ended in peace and economy. When the Government of Lord Salisbury entered office in 1895, the international horizon was so clear and cloudless that, early in the autumn, the Under Secretary for Foreign Affairs attributed the peaceful attitude of Europe to some sort of holy awe inspired by his chief, and seemed confident that an unexampled era of peaceful progress was at hand. The Jameson Raid, Armenia, Crete, Venezuela,

IMPERIALISM AND FINANCE

Siam, Madagascar, Omdurman, Fashoda, Indian Frontier, Uganda, are catch-words which recall an almost uninterrupted series of foreign troubles.

After a long period of trade depression (which had given an impetus to the protectionist and collectivist movements), the very first revenue declared by Sir Michael Hicks-Beach marked the beginning of a revival. The gross imperial revenue (*i.e.*, the revenue collected by the central authority) of the United Kingdom for the year ending March 31st, 1895, was £101,657,000.[1] Taxation remained practically unchanged until March 31st, 1898, so that the revenues of the next three years show the surpluses which Sir Michael Hicks-Beach would have realized if his expenditure had remained where it stood in the year ending March 31st, 1895:

		Surplus.
	£	£
Revenue for the year ending March 31, 1896	102,393,000	736,000
Revenue for the year ending March 31, 1897	112,154,000	10,497,000
Revenue for the year ending March 31, 1898	116,040,000	14,383,000

[1] I get this and the following figures by adding Table No. 13 to Table No. 2 of the Statistical Abstract in accordance with the note at the foot of p. 9. I thus include the imperial doles, *i.e.*, the amounts transferred after collection from imperial to local taxation.

LIBERALISM AND THE EMPIRE

In the 1898 Budget a small reduction was made in the tobacco duties, and income-tax abatements were extended; but the growth of the revenue, though checked, was not suspended.

		SURPLUS.
Revenue for the year ending March 31, 1899 ... ... £117,891,000		£16,234,000

In his Budget speech in the spring of 1899, the Chancellor of the Exchequer had to confess that the extravagance of the Government had at last outrun its prosperity. A deficit of £2,700,000 was estimated for the coming year. Two millions of this was filled up by a raid on the Sinking Fund, and the odd seven hundred thousand by increasing the wine duties and the stamp duties. Again the revenue exceeded all expectations, amounting in the year ended March 31st, 1900, to £129,757,000; surplus, £28,100,000.

Adding these five surpluses together, we get the monstrous total of £69,950,000. This is the gross sum which the Unionist Government had to spend up to March 31st, 1900, over and above what would have been needful if the costs of administration, and grants in aid of establishments had been maintained on the scale of 1894-95, the last year of office of the Liberal Government.

During these five years the income-tax stood still at 8d. An infinitesimal fraction (and that only for one year) of the surpluses went to relieve the payer of imperial taxes. How, then, did all the money vanish? How did the Chancellor of the Exchequer get rid of his enormous superfluities? In truth, Sir Michael would seem to have turned an old principle of medicine to political use. Four leeches have been applied to the body politic—the land leech, the Anglican leech, the naval leech, and the military leech. A few hundred thousand pounds only remained over for division between necessitous Board schools and the Post Office. So small are the reproductive investments of habitual prosperity when allied with systematic prodigality!

The millions which have been turned since 1897 from national purposes to the uses of landlords, Anglican clergymen, and voluntary schools certainly run far into double figures; but the Agricultural Rates Acts, the financial clauses of the Irish Local Government Act, the Tithe Rating Act and the grants to voluntary schools, bear so plainly the stamp of privilege and sectarianism, are so obviously dictated by the spirit of partisanship and monopoly, that the sordid details of these homely jobberies need not here be hunted out. They have been exposed in all their squalor by Parliament, press, and pamphlet. The opposition, brilliantly led by Sir William Harcourt, made its protests heard. When, in the spring of 1901, the Agricultural Rates Act expires, every man with a breath of Liberalism in his body will call out against its renewal.

I turn once more to the main item of expenditure

LIBERALISM AND THE EMPIRE

that it may be seen, in the words of Burke—and with what insistence, with what impressive gravity, would he have repeated them now!—'how necessary it is to review our military expenses for some years past, and, if possible, to bind up and close that bleeding artery of profusion.'

A fourth successful panic about armaments was worked up by Mr. Stead in the year 1883. He struck the match, and there was such an appearance of a popular blaze, that the editors all came running up with faggots and oil to warm their hands at the fire and improve their circulation. Mr. Gladstone's Government for some time poured water on the flames, but finally yielded in the Budget of 1884, and a large 'temporary' addition was made to the naval estimates. The press, no doubt, had much quiet but effective backing.

'A few anti-alarmists or sceptics,' says the 'Annual Register' for 1884, 'declared that the outcry in the newspapers was chiefly the work of the professional advisers of the Admiralty, assisted in a great measure by the large ship-builders whose yards were empty, and whose trade was temporarily at a standstill.'

On the completion of Lord Northbrook's programme in 1887, Lord Randolph Churchill,[1] then Chancellor of the Exchequer in the Unionist Government, resigned office, on the express ground that he could not persuade his colleagues to go back by

[1] In December, 1887.

steady reductions to the old standard of military and naval expenditure. He pointed out that an average of 25 millions annually had sufficed from 1874-84, that the average for the last three years had been more than 31 millions, and that the difference was equal to a permanent addition of 3d. to the income-tax. For this he held that there was no justification; a policy of 'effective retrenchment' was 'perfectly feasible'; it is 'quite unnecessary,' he said, to increase our armaments 'if the foreign policy of the country is conducted with skill and judgment.' His resignation was accepted, and Mr. Goschen took the vacant place.

From this time the naval estimates have never looked backwards. The sensational programme of 1884 was followed by the sensational programme of 1889.[1] The scheme proposed and begun by Lord Spencer in 1894 was supposed to put the navy into a position beyond the reach of criticism. It was given out that the demands of the ignorant agitator and the trained expert, of the patriotic contractor and of the octogenarian admiral, had at last attained finality. The taxpayer was to have a rest, or, rather, the revolutions of the agonizing wheel of taxation were not to be accelerated.

[1] Mr. Shaw-Lefevre's speech on the third reading of the Naval Defence Bill of 1889 is an admirable summary of the arguments against spasmodic and sensational additions to the navy.

LIBERALISM AND THE EMPIRE

Perhaps if Lord Spencer had remained in office these expectations might have been realized; perhaps the naval expenditure would have learned to remain as stationary as did the army expenditure under Sir Henry Campbell Bannerman's[1] firm and careful supervision. But unfortunately for the country, Lord Spencer was succeeded in 1895 by Mr. Goschen, whose love of ostentatious and aggressive outlay has made him a willing prey of the panicmonger and a passive instrument of the Navy League. Mr. Goschen's record is appalling.

EXPENDITURE ON THE NAVY.

For the year ending March 31, 1896	...	£19,724,000[2]
,, ,, ,, 1897	...	22,170,000
,, ,, ,, 1898	...	20,850,000
,, ,, ,, 1899	...	24,068,000
,, ,, ,, 1900	...	26,978,000

The estimates for the year ending March 31st, 1901, were introduced by Mr. Goschen as follows:

'When we took office five years ago the navy estimates stood at £18,700,000. To-day I propose them at £27,500,000—nearly half as much again. The average yearly increase during these years has been about £2,000,000, but the progress has not been uniform. On one occasion the leap that was

---

[1] The expenditure on the army stood at 17 millions odd so long as the Liberal Government (1892-95) was in office.

[2] An increase of more than two millions on the previous year.

IMPERIALISM AND FINANCE

taken amounted to £3,100,000; last year it was £2,800,000. . . . To the estimates this year of £27,500,000 must be added about £2,000,000, probably, for expenditure under the Naval Works Act, which, added to the other sum, would bring up the total to nearly £30,000,000 sterling. . . . I say this coldly, not rhetorically, for the information of the committee.'[1]

This is an admirably lucid summary of the financial aspect of aggressive imperialism so far as it relates to the navy. Mr. Goschen added that the estimates he was proposing were not sensational, and that the absence of a sensational increase had caused dissatisfaction in some quarters.

Whether the 'progress' and the average increase are or are not 'sensational' matters little. They are

[1] See *Times* Report, February 27th, 1900. This was one of several occasions when Mr. Goschen cracked the favourite Ministerial joke: 'It seems a very long time since the Hague Convention for mutual disarmament met. When that Convention was about to be called, Her Majesty's Government suggested that the laying down of further battleships might be kept in suspense with a view to ascertaining what the decision of the Convention might be. In the six months succeeding the Convention more gigantic programmes had been conceived and elaborated than had before apparently entered into the minds of the Powers.' (Laughter.) In the previous spring he had said that if foreign Governments would 'diminish' their shipbuilding schemes, Her Majesty's Government might consider the advisability of 'modifying' their programme.

unparalleled—they are out of all proportion to the advance in the prosperity of the country. It is mathematically certain that if the 'progress' continues a point will be reached in a few years at which the accumulation of war ships and war material will be stopped, if not by the taxable patience, then by the taxable capacity of the people. The only limit, however, upon which Mr. Goschen dwelt was that imposed by the dockyards. It would have been useless, he said, to propose larger estimates. No more orders could be placed. This statement grated upon the sensitive nerves of certain organ-voices which always sing private interests to the accompaniment of patriotic airs: 'God save the Queen and enrich Baron Glückchild,' 'Rule Britannia and ennoble Herr Oppenbeit.' That section of the press which identifies the interests of the contractors and the country naturally raised an indignant outcry; but it was a shock to read such a paragraph as the following in the political notes (not in the advertisement columns) of a newspaper so eminently respectable as the *Sunday Observer* :[1]

'It is understood that a public meeting will be held on March 28th in the Queen's Hall for the purpose of urging the Government to increase their naval preparations to a greater extent than was announced by the First Lord of the Admiralty in his speech on the navy estimates. Mr. Goschen's statements as to the im-

[1] For March 18th, 1900.

possibility of enlarging the programme of naval construction are not borne out by the facts. Messrs. Vickers, Son, and Maxim's yard at Barrow could undertake the construction of another battleship. Brown and Co. could take one. Palmer, on the Tyne, could certainly construct two large ships; while at Elswick Messrs. Armstrong could undertake three or four battleships or large cruisers. One large cruiser could be undertaken by Messrs. Earle, at Hull. In a word, if the Admiralty really want more ships, that is to say, if they were intent on carrying out their programme (which for eight years has not been done), eight additional ships would now be under construction. The existence of fifteen battleships armed with obsolete guns, the grave deficiency of cruisers, which are to the navy what cavalry and mounted infantry are to the army, the existence of inflammable fittings on all the older ships to such an extent that they would blaze like tar-barrels, the failure to prevent the export of steam-coal, and the presence of 35,000 foreigners in our merchant service, are matters of national concern on which the public is invited to express an opinion.'

The ordinary slow-thinking, right-minded citizen, for whom 'magnificent isolation' and splendid bankruptcy have no attractions, will think over these 'matters of national concern' in the light of the fact that the British fleet is more than equal to those of France and Russia combined, and will reflect that the income-tax might have been reduced to threepence or fourpence, or a sum of considerably more than thirty millions struck off the National Debt, if Mr. Goschen had been content to leave the naval estimates as he found them. Nor is it at all certain that if he had taken that course our naval predominance would have been less marked. For it is our expenditure which forces the pace. The spurts in our estimates have been followed, not preceded, by the spurts of the other Great Powers. Germany, France, and Russia refuse to be left further behind; and whenever an immense addition is made to our outlay, it is used as *the* argument (and a convincing one) to force a similar increase upon a reluctant Czar, a recalcitrant Reichstag, and an unwilling Chamber of Deputies. As these pages are being written, Count von Bülow is pushing his new Navy Bill through the Reichstag with arguments which are entirely built upon the growth of aggressive imperialism and aggressive armaments in England. In his first speech he gave a Prussian account of the change in British policy:

'From the time of the Napoleonic wars down to the seventies and eighties the policy of England was governed by the ideas of Adam Smith and John Bright and by the principle of non-intervention. To this period belonged the cession of the Ionian Islands, the abandonment of the Soudan, and the convention with the South African Republic after Majuba Hill. The imperialist movement now is constantly gaining ground.'

IMPERIALISM AND FINANCE

Accordingly he urged that Germany must increase her naval armaments with the object of securing peace and of giving the proper weight to her diplomacy. Herr Bassermann, a National Liberal, said bluntly that the reason for increasing the fleet was the necessity for strengthening the defences of Germany against England.

Even on purely fighting principles it would have been better for Great Britain to spend less and make sure of getting value for her money, instead of alarming the world by ostentatious extravagance, and spectacular demonstrations of naval superiority. Gold as well as iron is a 'main nerve' of war. Our war-chest would have been bigger if fleet had not been added to fleet and army to army. We should have had more strength in reserve and less hostility to encounter. Is it not probable that the real power as well as the popularity of Great Britain would have been greater if Ministers had been willing to follow Sir Robert Peel's example and 'run a little risk'?

'Do not beggar or cripple yourselves in war premiums on insurance against every contingency that an excited or imaginative soldier or sailor tells you may arise.'[1]

Ministers and people have forgotten Sir Robert Peel and flouted Mr. Morley's advice; but they will have to come back and give heed to both sooner or later.

[1] Mr. Morley at Leicester, March 23rd, 1898.

LIBERALISM AND THE EMPIRE

So long as Mr. Chamberlain is in power, Great Britain must be armed to the teeth. So long as aggressive imperialism is the policy of her Ministers, 'you may depend upon it,' to borrow the words of Sir William Harcourt, 'whatever you may say, whatever you may do, this increase of expenditure, not by hundreds of thousands, but by tens of millions,' will go on year after year, 'and must mean increased taxation.'

It will be objected that, if their country were not overinsured, the agitators would be dissatisfied; but they are dissatisfied as it is, even with Mr. Goschen. The alarm seems to grow with the expenditure. In the early months of 1900 the Jingoes wanted not only expenditure on a more lavish scale, but also a press-gang for the navy and conscription for the army. It was suddenly discovered that half the ships of the Royal Navy are 'death-traps.' The Navy League redoubled its exertions, and formulated a fresh series of demands, so startling in their extravagance as to call down rebukes from the editorial chairs of the Jingo press. In one of the February debates in the House of Commons, Admiral Field shouted to the captains and colonels of the other service to follow the example set by his own in panicmongering.

'Get some of your distinguished generals to do that; get the press on your side. The South African Expedition would have been impossible in 1884. Our

IMPERIALISM AND FINANCE

agitation has produced an invincible navy. Agitate, then.'

Imagine any other highly-paid service in the world whose officers are commissioned to perambulate the country touting for orders! Shortly afterwards it was announced in the *Times* that 'Service' Committees had been appointed in both Houses 'to secure concerted action on questions affecting the navy, the army, and the auxiliary forces.'

Meanwhile, the army expenditure, left by Sir Henry Campbell Bannerman at £17,973,000, already showed in the four years ending March 31st, 1899, an advance disproportionately greater than that made by British exports to foreign countries and the colonies during the same period. The figures are:

For the year ending March 31, 1896 ...	£18,428,000
,, ,, ,, 1897 ...	18,152,000
,, ,, ,, 1898 ...	19,348,000
,, ,, ,, 1899 ...	20,018,000

But this is a very inadequate account of the demands made by the War Office upon the public purse. Look a little lower down the table (No. 3 of the Statistical Abstract), and you will come upon further items stowed away under the unobtrusive heading 'Issues to meet Other Expenditure.'

Under this head the expenditure in 1894 and 1895 amounted to between £800,000 and £900,000. Now mark its expansion in the four years which follow:

LIBERALISM AND THE EMPIRE

	1896.	1897.	1898.	1899.
	£	£	£	£
Under Imperial Defence Act, 1888	58,000	...	...	...
Under Barracks Act, 1890	600,000	320,000	300,000	200,000
Under Telegraph Acts	572,000	138,000	160,000	133,000
Under Naval Works Acts	860,000	905,000	596,000	1,080,000
Under Public Offices Act, 1895	...	95,000	325,000	30,000
Under Uganda Railway Act, 1896	...	366,000	595,000	1,005,000
Under Public Offices Act, 1897	...	...	25,000	475,000
Under Military Works Act, 1897	...	...	750,000	630,000
Under Public Buildings Act, 1898	...	...	...	2,550,000
Total	2,090,000	1,824,000	2,751,000	6,103,000

Working men with a pretty taste for public buildings or a large telegraphic correspondence may find a modicum of consolation in these figures, and the income-tax payer who contributes so much and receives so little may comfort himself by the reflection that there must be many contractors whose homes have been brightened and whose purses have been lined out of the spoils. Our figures only carry us to the spring of 1899, before the idea of 'wiping out the Boers' or 'mopping up the mines' had struck

IMPERIALISM AND FINANCE

the Ministerial imagination. Indeed, the British army was getting so little exercise that Lord Lansdowne thought it proper to induce the Chancellor of the Exchequer to effect, on behalf of the nation, a compulsory purchase of Salisbury Plain from Sir Michael Hicks-Beach and other landlords. The Plain seems to have been very cheap strategically, and very dear agriculturally.[1]

The army estimates for 1899-1900 were also framed under peaceful conditions, and should therefore be added in this place; they indicate a fresh growth in Lord Lansdowne's conception of 'a normal increase.' They were practically 22 millions—to be quite exact, £21,978,000—an estimated increase of nearly two millions upon the army expenditure of 1898-99, and of four millions upon the army expenditure of 1894-95. These estimates alarmed some of the sober men among the Ministerialists. Nor was their dismay surprising, considering the promises of Old Age Pensions and other costly reforms which had been scattered broadcast at the General Election of 1895. They saw the fifth great surplus engulfed in a military and naval expenditure which had risen close upon 40 per cent. since the advent of Lord Salisbury to power. Nevertheless, when the army estimates came to be discussed, it was from the Opposition alone that the

---

[1] See Mr. T. G. Bowles's letters and those of valuers and solicitors connected with the transaction in the *Times* during the autumn months of 1899.

demand came for reduction in the expenditure, Mr. Courtenay Warner urging that the nation should get more value for its money.

'There is one thing at the outset that we have to make a protest against, and that is the whole system of expenditure in connection with the army. We contend that that system might be very much improved, and effect greater results than at present for less money.'

And he added, speaking as a moderate Liberal who had got up his subject:

'My friends on this side are not in any way wedded to any particular form of economy; but . . . we realize that, the estimates having reached above 21 millions, the country will not stand any more expenditure, and the day will come when a very serious reduction in the army and its efficiency will be demanded, unless something is done to manage the army on a more economic system than we have at the present moment. . . . Most of us regret that the army will have to be increased in the future, in order to occupy the large tracts of territory which have been added to the Empire, and which additions are very unlikely to pay for many years to come. But once these large tracts of territory have been acquired, we foresee that, unless something is done to modify the present expensive system, the expenditure will go on increasing by leaps and bounds.'[1]

[1] See Hansard, March 17th, 1899.

IMPERIALISM AND FINANCE

A month later Sir Michael Hicks-Beach made a similar prediction:

'Now, sir, I think one thing is quite clear, and that is that it is impossible, however great the prosperity of the country may be, for such increases as this—of £5,000,000 or £6,000,000 a year in our expenditure—to be met by mere automatic increase of our existing taxation, nor could they be met for long by any increase of existing taxes. If this rate of increase is to continue, Parliament and the country must make up their minds not only to large increases in the existing taxes, but also to the discovery of new and productive sources of revenue.'[1]

It is, unfortunately, only too plain, from the sentences which follow, that Sir Michael Hicks-Beach had flung to the winds the best traditions of his office:

'I will venture to prophesy that the result of this will necessarily be a reaction against this great expenditure, which no one would deplore more than I should; for I am convinced that the result of such a reaction would be to reduce the efficiency and the strength of our defensive services to the point at which they unhappily stood in the last generation.'

Mr. Gladstone once described the office now held by Sir Michael Hicks-Beach as 'never a very popular one,' because a very large part of the Minister's time is spent in saying to those who demand public expenditure, 'No, no, no.' A famous Colonial Premier

[1] Sir M. Hicks-Beach, Hansard, April 13th, 1899.

LIBERALISM AND THE EMPIRE

has been nicknamed 'Yes-No.' Sir Michael is the 'Yes, yes, yes' Chancellor of the Exchequer.

A Minister deploring a reaction which he predicts from a prodigality for which he is responsible lays himself open to criticism from every quarter. But the most fervent imperialist sees that the time is at hand when the nation will choose the policy of the future by giving its verdict on the past. 'We have come to the parting of the ways.' The addition of more than 13 millions in five years to our naval and military estimates is a grievous annual drain upon the wealth of the country; for it represents a capital sum of 500 millions withdrawn from industry. This vast sum had been locked up and the interest on it ear-marked for unproductive expenditure before the outbreak of the South African War. If the war, as well as the permanent additions to our warlike establishments, had been avoided, the sum annually saved would almost have paid the interest on the National Debt; or the income-tax, instead of being increased to a shilling, might have been decreased to a penny.

Plainly the Unionist party is pledged to further sensational instalments of militarism, and provocative armaments. Ministers frankly claim credit for the past, and admit that their future aims may be judged by their actions since they took office in 1895. At any rate, their record stands undisputed. The question for the country is whether it shall be blamed or praised. Dark as the outlook

IMPERIALISM AND FINANCE

appears to be, it cannot be doubted that a great future awaits that portion of the Liberal Party which, setting its face against the wasteful excesses of aggressive imperialism, repudiating conscription in all its forms, is resolutely determined to maintain the superiority of our fleet at the proportions fixed by tradition and reason, and to improve without increasing an army whose vast cost contrasts so ludicrously with its efficiency; is convinced above all of the utter hopelessness of attempting by any conceivable inflation of military establishments to force upon the world indefinite pretensions of race and empire, and identifies itself with a firm, civilized, and studiously unaggressive policy.

II

So far discussion has been confined to our calculated panics about armaments and our incalculable expenditure upon them. Other elements hitherto excluded must now be introduced. It requires no economist to discern that expenditure on war is far worse than military expenditure in time of peace. The armaments of peace turn wealth into unproductive channels; war turns wealth to the purposes of destroying wealth. As these lines are being written, Great Britain is spending two or three million sovereigns a week in wholesale destruction of men, horses, cattle, and capital of all kinds in her own colonies or in States immediately contiguous, whose prosperity reacts upon her own. I do not know that any writer has ever succeeded in analyzing the finance of war. But Mr. Bright once flashed out in his imaginative way a profound aphorism. One of the advantages of war, he wrote, is that you can have a very little for a very great deal of money. The truth might be illustrated by an examination of the causes of the rise of the National Debt or of the fluctuations of the income-tax. A partial explanation is suggested by Mr. Gladstone's dictum that 'war suspends, *ipso facto*, every rule of public thrift,' and 'tends to sap honesty itself in the use of public treasure, for which it makes such unbounded calls.'

What a storm was raised but lately against the Treasury for being suspected of having performed its duty of scrutinizing and criticizing the national accounts in those summer months when contractors were already beginning to batten on the prospective picnic to Pretoria! In the black month of February, 1900, when the Rhodesian and Chamberlainite press was hunting with feverish energy for some scapegoat outside the sacred circle of international finance and its local instruments and agents, the Prime Minister himself stooped to attack the most competent department of Government in a mean attempt to throw off from the shoulders of himself and his colleagues on to the shoulders of subordinates the charge of unpreparedness and the responsibility for miscalculation and failure. He said that Treasury control led to 'much delay and many doubtful resolutions.' But the Premier's Rhodesian fury was short-lived.

'Quickly he repented what he had rashly done.'

He made an apology, abject and complete, first to the Chancellor of the Exchequer, then to the permanent staff of the Treasury. The hunt for victims proved a failure. The cowardly hue-and-cry dropped whenever the selected victim showed his teeth.[1] It was felt that any enquiry might disclose the real culprits and bring the merits of the war and its promoters before the eye of the people.

This particular contest in which our country is now engaged seems indeed to have been intended by Providence for a great object-lesson in what we have called Financial Imperialism. 'One inevitable characteristic of modern war,' wrote Mr. Gladstone in 1859, after first directing as Minister then criticizing in Opposition the finances of a mighty conflict with Russia, 'is that it is associated throughout in all its particulars with a vast and most irregular formation of commercial enterprise.'

[1] Perhaps the most organized and persistent attacks were those upon Sir Michael Hicks-Beach and Sir William Butler. Sir Michael Hicks-Beach's real crime was that he had proposed to tax the gold-mines. Sir William Butler had not only advised against the plan of triangular defence, but acquainted the Home Government with the hollowness and insincerity of the Uitlander agitation.

LIBERALISM AND THE EMPIRE

'There is no incentive to Mammon-worship so remarkable as that which it affords. The political economy of war is now one of its most commanding aspects. Every farthing, with the smallest exceptions conceivable, of the scores or hundreds of millions which a war may cost goes directly, and very violently, to stimulate production, though it is intended ultimately for waste or destruction. . . . It is the greatest feeder of that lust of gold which we are told is the essence of commerce, though we had hoped it was only its besetting sin.' But this is not the whole case. Mr. Gladstone added that 'the regular commerce of peace is tameness itself compared with the gambling spirit which war, through the rapid shiftings and high prices which it brings, always introduces into trade.' He thought that war in its moral operations 'more resembles, perhaps, the finding of a new gold-field than anything else.'

In our war with the two republics no detail is wanting to complete this picture. We see a fight for gold-fields introduced by gambling. Kaffirs as well as consols fluctuate with every change in its fortunes. Bears and bulls let loose their alternate rumours; and every fresh outpouring of blood is foreshadowed and recorded in a rise or fall of Stock Exchange securities. You have quotations before and after a skirmish, failures and fortunes after a defeat, failures and fortunes after a victory. Long Tom's discharges reverberate in every synagogue of Europe and America.

IMPERIALISM AND FINANCE

It will be useful for the purposes of this essay to set the South African conflict in its financial environment, in order that the conditions to which Liberal principles will have to be applied may be better understood, that it may be seen how finance can be fought by finance, jobbery by policy, and how the underground operations of private capitalists may be countermined by the searching processes of the tax-gatherer and the relentless supervision of the administrator. An average citizen, who votes at an election, who says of a thing 'it is true because I read it in the paper,' is so proud of his country that he is slow to believe his Government can commit a crime. Great Britain and Greater Britain are very dear to him. He never dreams that an Empire so magnificent, and once so magnanimous, can be ruled by little minds, and that those little minds may be swayed by sordid motives. He understands the ways and means of the local swindler, he may have profited by one 'combine' and lost by another, he may know something of the corrupt influences that are sometimes brought to bear upon the action of his own town council; but he is very loath to enlarge his experience and inspect the International in the light of the Parochial Rogue. The Queen's Ministry, the Privy Council, the Houses of Parliament—can these august bodies be liable to vulgar sins and human infirmities? No! It is unthinkable.

Now, it happens that among the members of Her

LIBERALISM AND THE EMPIRE

Majesty's Privy Council there is a certain Right Honourable Cecil Rhodes. This man is not only in the technical sense 'right honourable,' but has done nothing to affect his personal honour in the expressed opinion of Her Majesty's Secretary of State for the Colonies. The *Times* described him a little while ago as the 'personification of imperialism.' He is so learned in the Companies Acts that the University of Oxford has granted him the title of Doctor of Civil Law. You may picture him if you like in Grootschur, his country palace, fingering Dutch curios or toying with his type-written translations of the classics. Now the zoologist may stroll out for half an hour to feed his lions, or the horticulturist to tend his roses, but soon the ardent student is again in his library, buried in Gibbon, whom he has got 'almost by heart.'[1] Is this the page he is half reading, half reciting?—

'The legal incorporation of these societies by the charters of popes and kings had given them a monopoly of the public instruction. And the spirit of monopolists is narrow, lazy, and oppressive; their work is more costly and less productive than that of independent artists; and the new improvements, so eagerly grasped by the competition of freedom, are admitted with slow and sullen reluctance in those proud corporations, above the fear of a rival and below the confession of an error. We may scarcely hope that any reformation will be a

---

[1] See Rhodes, Cecil, in 'Who's Who?' (1900).

IMPERIALISM AND FINANCE

voluntary act; and so deeply are they rooted in law and prejudice that even the omnipotence of Parliament would shrink from an inquiry into the state and abuses of [the two Universities].'[1]

Poor Gibbon! His petulance was inexcusable. He must have seen clearly the advantages of a charter of incorporation—for those who are incorporated, and of a monopoly—for the monopolist. The pupil is unquestionably greater than his master. The 'empire-builder' excels the author of the 'Decline and Fall,' for instead of railing vainly against abuses and privileges, he secures and benefits by them. This sprig of the Oriel fathers is more prodigious than that offshoot from the monks of Magdalen. It was in the seventies that Mr. Rhodes began to make money and connections in the Kimberley diamond-fields. In the early eighties he was already in the Cape Parliament, occupied partly in opposing the Imperial factor and conciliating the Dutch, but mainly in preparing for a great financial coup in Kimberley. At last, in the year 1888, the whole Kimberley group of competing diamond companies had been swallowed up in De Beers; and Mr. Rhodes, as manager of De Beers, was in receipt of a princely income, had four seats in the Cape Parliament absolutely at his disposal, as well as a big secret service fund provided for in the trust-deeds of the new company. The legality of this

[1] Gibbon's Autobiography, 1814 edition, p. 49.

consolidation of the diamond-mines was questioned in the Cape Courts in 1888, and the Chief Justice's judgment helps us to some conception of the powers then acquired and now exercised by De Beers.

'It is quite true,' he said, 'that one of the purposes for which the De Beers Company was established is diamond-mining; but that forms an insignificant portion of the powers which may be exercised by the company. The company can undertake financial arrangements for foreign governments; may carry on diamond-mining, gold-mining, and coal-mining in any part of the world; it can carry on banking in Africa or elsewhere; and become a water company in the colony or elsewhere. In point of fact, it is of public note that an Act has been passed this session empowering the De Beers Company to perform the duties of a water company. The powers of the company are as extensive as those of any company that ever existed.'

De Beers has also got the sole right to diamonds up to the Zambesi, including any possible discoveries in German territory. It has many thousand square miles of land in the north and in British Bechuanaland. In 1891 De Beers secured the Wesselton diamond-mine by an especially shady job (Mr. Rhodes being then Prime Minister); and a little later the Indwe coal-mine fell into its clutches.[1]

[1] For more information on these points and on the powers and tyranny of De Beers see 'Capital and Labour: the Supreme Problem in South Africa,' by H. C. Thomson; reprinted from *The Investors' Review*.

IMPERIALISM AND FINANCE

Enormous profits to the directors and shareholders of De Beers accompanied the reduction of Kimberley to the condition of industrial and political servitude in which it still subsists.[1] This monopoly, which has been able not only to reduce the wages of black and white miners in Kimberley far below the level of Johannesburg, but also to raise and maintain the price of diamonds, was the creation of a group of international financiers, working through, and inspired by the genius of, Mr. Rhodes. The influence of this group in the Cape Parliament consolidated their conquest by legalizing the compound system and exempting the diamond-mines from taxation.

With friends and co-operators like Messrs. Barnato, Beit, and Eckstein, Mr. Rhodes was now able to test still more thoroughly the truth of that venerable saying, 'Every man (and every newspaper) has his price.'

Encouraged by the achievement of Kimberley, and by some minor successes over Imperial officers, he proceeded to form a new scheme, which required a visit to London and an application to metropolitan society of the same methods which had been found effectual in Cape Town. Vainly had Adam Smith warned British statesmen that exclusive companies are bad for commerce but worse for empires, and vainly had his warnings been written out in the chapter and verse of bitter experience. The great publicist has told of

[1] The population of Kimberley has been reduced by one-half since this monopoly in diamonds was created.

LIBERALISM AND THE EMPIRE

'the oppressive and monopolizing spirit which is natural to the directors of a regulated company;' he has observed that the genius of these companies is 'unfavourable to the growth of new colonies.' To no purpose. Avidity still overrules statesmanship, and endangers empire with the Black Magic of Imperialism. A cheque of £10,000 paid by Mr. Rhodes into the Irish Home Rule Funds secured the sympathies of the Nationalist party and of Mr. Parnell, without leading a Unionist Government to suspect the character of Mr. Rhodes's Imperial patriotism. No Parliamentary inquiry was granted; no Parliamentary debate was allowed. Baron de Worms was put up to give evasive replies to inconvenient questions; and at the end of the session of 1889, by an exercise of a prerogative of the Crown, on a petition signed by Mr. Rhodes, a native of Hamburg, and one or two noble decoy-ducks, a Royal Charter was granted to the British[1] South Africa Company to exploit the vast territory of Rhodesia. This was the first act in a new South African tragedy.

'Whereas,' so ran the preamble to this charter, 'the said petition states . . . that the existence of a powerful

[1] There is a quaint clause in the charter providing that directors of the company should be British subjects, *but that this provision should not apply to any person named as director in the charter who did not fulfil the condition.* It was a little awkward that the charter could not speak of 'our loyal subjects.'

IMPERIALISM AND FINANCE

British company controlled by these of our subjects in whom we have confidence . . . would be advantageous to the commercial and other interests of our subjects . . . [and] that the petitioners desire to carry into effect divers concessions and agreements which have been made by certain of the chiefs and tribes inhabiting the said region, and such other concessions, agreements, grants, and treaties as the petitioners may hereafter obtain within the said region or elsewhere in Africa, with the view of promoting trade, commerce, civilization and good government (including the regulation of liquor-traffic with the natives) . . . [and] that the petitioners believe that if the said concessions, agreements, grants, and treaties can be carried into effect, the condition of the natives inhabiting the said territories will be materially improved and their civilization advanced. . . . Now, therefore, we . . . being satisfied that the intentions of the petitioners are praiseworthy and deserve encouragement, and that the enterprise in the petition described may be productive of the benefits set forth therein, by our prerogative royal and of our especial grace, certain knowledge and mere motion, have constituted, erected, and incorporated, and by this our Charter for us and our heirs and royal successors do constitute, erect, and incorporate into one body politic and corporate by the name of the British South Africa Company the said James, Duke of Abercorn, Alexander William George, Duke of Fife, Edric Frederic, Lord Gifford, Cecil John Rhodes, Alfred Beit, Albert Henry George Grey, and George Cawston, and such other persons,' etc.

LIBERALISM AND THE EMPIRE

Within a few months the one million original shares had been syndicated, and the right to apply for the £1 shares of the new issue sold for £4 a share. So that a present of the value of £3,000,000 had already been made to the grantees of the Charter. It is exactly the case on a large scale of the man who gets by favour of the justices a new license for a public-house.

The next development may be given in the words of a writer whose competence and accuracy will scarcely be questioned :

'By 1893 it was pretty plainly seen that the company was a financial failure. Its shares were quoted at barely above par,[1] and it had become clear that there was no gold worth speaking of to be obtained in Mashonaland. At the same time, reports began to be circulated that, though there might be no gold in Mashonaland, there was plenty to be had in Matabeleland. About the same time, moreover, reports began to be circulated that the Matabele chief, Lo Bengula, whose conduct up to then had been universally praised,[2] was getting "cheeky," and would have to be settled with. By methods which are well understood in South Africa, and which ought to be now better understood in England, a pretext for a quarrel with Lo Bengula was manufactured. By means of organized misrepresentation and judicious use of the telegraph-wires, it came to be believed in this country

[1] *Rhodesia Herald*, October 27, 1893.
[2] *Ibid.*, December 10, 1892.

IMPERIALISM AND FINANCE

that the settlers in Mashonaland were in imminent danger of being wiped out by a "horde" of savages. ("Horde" is a very effective word in connection with enterprises of this kind.) The Chartered Company's forces invaded Matabeleland, and by great good luck managed to seize Bulawayo with trifling loss. The event, according to the enthusiastic language of the leading newspaper in Rhodesia, "changed the face of heaven and earth."[1] A brisk business was immediately done in Chartered Company's shares at an enhanced price, while in England the additional capital that was needed to mend the rents in the company's financial garments was raised without difficulty.[2] The fact that some thousands of Matabele lost their lives, as well as a detachment of gallant Europeans, was of little importance in the opposite scale. Such an appearance of prosperity was created that the chief holders of Chartered Company's shares were able a little later to unload them upon the public at a heavy profit.'[3]

The amount of this profit can only be estimated roughly by comparing the shares held by the Rhodesian group in July, 1895, with the shares held by the same group afterwards in March, 1896. Between these dates the Jameson Raid occurred. In the October before the Raid 'Chartereds' stood at 8. A month after the Raid they were bought and

[1] *Rhodesia Herald*, November 10, 1893.
[2] *Ibid.*, November 17, 1893.
[3] See 'Mr. Rhodes and the Empire' (published by the *Morning Leader*), p. 22.

LIBERALISM AND THE EMPIRE

sold at less than half that figure. In July, 1895, Mr. Rhodes had 166,057 shares in his sole name, and Mr. Beit 122,376. In March, 1896, they held 29,463 and 7,496 shares respectively. In the same interval the firm of Beit and Rhodes had sold 209,491 shares. Other firms in which Mr. Rhodes and Mr. Beit were interested (the Beit Syndicate, Beit and Cawston, Rhodes and Beit, Rhodes, Rudd and Beit, and Goldfields of South Africa) also unloaded. The profits realized by some of the principal shareholders from these operations have been calculated[1] on a moderate basis as follows :

Name.	Profit.
Duke of Abercorn	£14,324
Duke of Fife	14,708
Earl Grey	27,612
Lord Gifford	38,388
Sir Horace Farquhar	60,928
Mr. Rhodes	546,376[2]
Mr. Beit	459,520
Mr. Rochfort Maguire	228,860
Goldfields of South Africa	477,108
Lord Rothschild	167,596
Beit and Rhodes (in joint names)	837,964[2]
Rhodes and Beit (in joint names)	45,600[2]
Rhodes, Rudd, and Beit	63,000[2]

[1] By Mr. Labouchere, whose exposures of the South African gang in the House of Commons and in *Truth* give him a claim to the gratitude of his countrymen.

[2] Compare Mr. Rhodes' speech to his shareholders, *Times*, May 2, 1900 : 'I should have liked to take more [than

IMPERIALISM AND FINANCE

I need not describe the Jameson Raid, which constitutes the third act of the tragedy. Made possible by the change of Government in England, its conception and execution was due to the triple powers of Mr. Rhodes over Rhodesia, De Beers, and the Cape. When the chief villain of the piece was let off, and his agents, local and Imperial, left untouched or visited with trifling punishments as a prelude to further promotion, Dutch suspicion of Mr. Chamberlain's complicity deepened into certainty. Even Mr. Lecky saw the trail of the financial serpent.

Now, supposing that so powerful a group of speculators, with such unlimited resources, and such political connections, hit upon a policy which they wanted the Imperial Government to pursue in South Africa, and supposing they hit upon it in the spring of 1899; supposing, further, that they had acquired control of the whole English press in South Africa with one exception, and supposing that the telegraphic news was dressed or concocted by their agents, and that this news found the majority of London editors and sub-editors ready to receive it and to give the policy resolved upon by our coterie of millionaires the impress of popular favour—granted all this, would the fact that such a policy was calculated to end in an unjust and unnecessary war dispose

---

200,000 shares]; but during the last ten years I have devoted myself to politics; and politics and the accumulation of money do not run together.'

an Imperial Government (formed, it should be remembered, from the same elements, and mainly composed of the same men, that had granted the Charter) to resist so tremendous a combination? If the reader to whom this question is addressed be inclined to answer in the negative, he will be met by an objection advanced by Sir Henry Fowler (in April, 1900), and one or two other prominent members of the Liberal Party: 'It cannot be a capitalists' war, because the capitalists will not gain by it.' To this there would seem to be a complete reply. The question is not whether the capitalists who have held on since the autumn of 1899 will eventually gain if they continue to hold on, but whether they expected to benefit by the policy of war. Now, that they anticipated a vast increase of dividends from the termination of Boer Government on the Rand (and still more, perhaps, from the exploitation of other gold-fields in the Transvaal) is shown conclusively, not only in Mr. Fitzpatrick's book, but also by many official statements made in the year 1899 by directors and experts at meetings of shareholders in the principal companies affected. Several millions were to be saved annually by the reduction of black and white wages, by facilitating the importation of niggers, and by introducing some form of compulsory labour for the blacks on the Kimberley or Rhodesian pattern. But the most convincing answer of all is by a simple reference to the fact that these anticipa-

IMPERIALISM AND FINANCE

tions were realized. Speculators who bought on a large scale at the end of September, 1899, and sold towards the end of November, made fortunes almost beyond the dreams of avarice. Take a few quotations at four different dates—the first before hostilities began, when speculators were still afraid that their hopes of war might yet be shattered, the third when all promised well, the fourth after the disasters:

	October 3, 1899.	October 20, 1899.	November 23, 1899.	January 31, 1900.
East Rand...	$4\frac{7}{8}$	$7\frac{1}{4}$	$7\frac{3}{4}$	$5\frac{5}{8}$
Rand Mines	$27\frac{1}{2}$	$38\frac{1}{4}$	$42\frac{5}{8}$	$30\frac{3}{4}$
Goldfields ...	$5\frac{1}{4}$	$7\frac{1}{2}$	$8\frac{1}{16}$	$6\frac{3}{16}$
Charltereds	$2\frac{5}{16}$	$3\frac{1}{3}$	$4\frac{1}{16}$	3
Modders ...	$7\frac{1}{2}$	$10\frac{1}{2}$	$11\frac{3}{8}$	$7\frac{7}{16}$

It might, however, very well be argued that the war in South Africa, though undoubtedly a flotation by speculators for speculators, was also a grand Imperial venture. The apparent interests of the British Empire and of the international financiers —so runs the argument—happened to coincide. If Imperialists and speculators alike made a miscalculation, so much the worse for both[1]; but the Empire

[1] Mr. Rhodes told the world in the summer of 1899 that there was an easy way with President Kruger. It is probable that Mr. Chamberlain was duped, and took the course which ended in war in the full belief that it would end in a peaceful and impressive humiliation of President Kruger.

LIBERALISM AND THE EMPIRE

has no stronger case against the speculators than the speculators against the Empire.

When a cruel wave of war, sweeping round the compounds of Kimberley, intercepted and incarcerated the Colossus on one of his visits to Bulawayo, it was very soon discovered that there is at least one man who regards the British army in South Africa simply as the instrument of the mining corporations which he controls. 'It is scandalous! It is simply monstrous!' he declared to Mr. Julian Ralph immediately after the siege. 'In heaven's name, why was it not done sooner?' Thrice was it necessary to postpone the annual meeting of the De Beers Company. Mr. Rhodes' sarcastic speeches and leading articles after Modder River and Magersfontein were so bitter that Colonel Kekewich threatened a court-martial. His conduct at Kimberley (and elsewhere) is best explained perhaps by that characteristic speech which described the British flag as 'a commercial asset.' The service and convenience of De Beers were made the sole test of military efficiency. A few great shareholders and speculators had given the British Government (one of their largest agencies) a big job to execute. There were, no doubt, elaborate specifications, but the contract itself was simple: 'We give a press and public opinion: you give an army.' The whole cost of military operations was to be at the outside £10,000,000, and it was agreed that, if a popular outcry should arise, a fraction might be

IMPERIALISM AND FINANCE

paid by the mining interest. It never occurred to either of the high contracting parties that a handful of peasants would fight for their independence, and that another handful of peasants would fulfil a treaty-obligation. And so, when unsuspected disasters occurred, when the war was prolonged, and its cost grew from 10 to 23, and from 23 to 63 millions, the relations between the Government and the syndicate became a little strained. The press was let loose against Mr. Balfour (who complained of the Raid) and against Sir Michael Hicks-Beach, who talked of taxing the gold-mines. For a few days it really seemed possible that certain Ministers would have to be ejected, and a friendly Government of national defence set up. A British Ministry floated by an international syndicate! Why not? The project may have been dropped, but it is perfectly feasible so long as the people upon whose will a Government depends runs in blinkers.

How is a democracy to know or even to suspect that its Ministers are a row of puppets, and that a board of international financiers sitting in Paris or Berlin or London pulls the wires, especially if that same board controls a great part of the press? The acquisition of the Charter, the Matabele War, and the Raid are three extraordinary proofs of the powers wielded by this unsuspected ring and of the modes in which these powers have been exercised. Another is furnished by the rehabilitation of Mr. Rhodes after the Raid.

LIBERALISM AND THE EMPIRE

Before the Raid, Rhodesia—an area of 750,000 square miles (more than twice the size of France or Germany)—was under the sole control of the financial group which obtained the Charter. From this group, to borrow the words used by the Duke of Abercorn to the South African Committee, 'Mr. Rhodes had received a power of attorney to do precisely what he liked without consultation with the Board; and the whole of the administration, and everything connected with the administration of Rhodesia, was carried on by Mr. Rhodes, he simply notifying to the Board what was done.' Wielding this vast, though irregular despotism, our typical Imperialist was at the same time a Privy Councillor, Prime Minister of the Cape, Managing Director and Life-Governor of De Beers, and, I think, Managing Director of the Consolidated Goldfields of South Africa. The duties of a Privy Councillor, as defined by his oath of office, are, to the best of his discretion, duly and impartially to advise the Queen, to keep secret her counsel, to avoid corruption, to strengthen the Queen's Council in all that is thought good for the Queen and her land, to withstand those who attempt the contrary, and to do all that a true councillor ought to do to his Sovereign. Bound by this oath and by obligations of honour equally stringent to his colleagues in the Cape Ministry, Mr. Rhodes secretly entered into a conspiracy and planned the Raid. A Committee of the House of Commons

IMPERIALISM AND FINANCE

decided, in a report signed by Mr. Chamberlain, Sir William Harcourt, Sir M. Hicks-Beach, and Sir Henry Campbell Bannerman, that the Raid did 'grave injury to British influence in South Africa,' that 'race-feeling was greatly embittered' thereby, that 'serious difficulties were created with neighbouring States,' and that the author of the Raid was Mr. Rhodes. 'His proceedings resulted in the invasion of the territory of a State which was in friendly relations, in breach of an obligation to respect the right of self-government of the South African Republic under the Convention between Her Majesty and that State.' What action did the Imperial Government take? Two years were allowed to elapse, and in the spring of 1898 the hero of these exploits, unrepentant, but forgiven, was allowed by Mr. Chamberlain to resume the administration of Rhodesia.[1] But perhaps his personal

[1] In the spring of 1898 Lord Grey went to Mr. Chamberlain and asked whether, if the Chartered Company re-elected Mr. Rhodes as director, the British Government would exercise its power of veto. Mr. Chamberlain gave the required assurance. The danger and wickedness of this step was pointed out by Sir Robert Reid in the House of Commons. 'I thought,' he said (on May 6, 1898), 'that the policy for which the whole House expressed its preference was that of reconciling the two governing races, the Dutch and the British, by avoiding on either side anything in the least tending towards irritation, of letting bygones be bygones, and in this way healing the wounds of the past.

LIBERALISM AND THE EMPIRE

conduct had redeemed in some degree his political vices. We turn again to the Committee's report. 'He (Mr. Rhodes) deceived the High Commissioner.' 'He concealed his views from his colleagues in the Colonial Ministry and from the board of the British South African Company . . . and led his subordinates to believe that his plans were approved by his superiors.'

The relations between Mr. Rhodes and Mr. Chamberlain are involved in a disreputable mist which neither party seems anxious to disperse. It would seem that Mr. Chamberlain has whitewashed Mr. Rhodes in order that Mr. Rhodes may refrain from blackmailing Mr. Chamberlain. But if a silvery mist, only a little lifted by the publication of a few letters from the Hawksley dossier, hangs over Mr. Chamberlain and Mr. Rhodes, a thick auriferous fog obscures the minor fluctuations, though not the larger movements, in the fixed ratio mintage of aggressive Imperialism and speculative finance.

An impartial eye-witness of the annual meeting

Will the policy of restoring Mr. Rhodes to the directorate of the Chartered Company be likely to tend in that direction? I venture to think that it will tend not only to produce irritation, but to retard the growth of that good feeling which all members of this House are desirous to see promoted with regard to foreign countries as well as the Transvaal, where our protests of innocence are accepted too often, I am afraid, with laughter.'

IMPERIALISM AND FINANCE

of the National Liberal Federation, held at Nottingham in the early spring of 1900, declared that, wide as were the differences of opinion there made manifest, one sentiment ran fiercely through the whole gathering. He summed it up in the phrase 'Fight the financiers!' May the Liberal party accept the omen, and may the battle be joined not only with militarism and the pure spirit of aggressive jingoism, but with the impure, corrupt, and degrading influences which are summed up in the name 'Financial Imperialism.' It is not possible to exaggerate the dangers which menace us from these sources. Börsen-politik is bad enough in domestic affairs; but when we find the Empire put in motion by foreigners for foreigners, it is time to counterwork the busy, though unseen, agencies of international finance. By the quiet purchase of half a dozen honest papers with a large circulation, and by a gentle, gradual reversal of their policy, something that looks remarkably like public opinion can be fabricated. When that is done, a free people cannot be said to enjoy freedom of the press. If news is carefully subedited,[1] and then a glowing leader

[1] The power of the sub-editor is considerable. In the *Times* of March 14, 1900, there appeared the following telegram (Reuter) : 'When the rebels entered Van Wyk's Vlei yesterday morning, Miss Walton, the postmistress, refused to give up the keys of the post-office. The rebels pointed a gun at her, and threatened to shoot her if she persisted in her

LIBERALISM AND THE EMPIRE

written upon doctored facts, a popular indignation is aroused by atrocities which never took place, and wrong impressions are formed which it is very difficult to erase. Consider how many Liberals who did not know of those changes in the editorship and ownership of the *Daily News* which took place some few years ago were insensibly drawn to palliate British inaction in regard to the Armenian massacres, to wink at the shameful abuse of the British navy in Crete, to join in an outcry for war with France over the swamps of Fashoda, and finally to see the pure spirit of patriotism and imperialism working through Mr. Rhodes, Mr. Beit, Mr. Eckstein, Mr. Garrett, and the rest, for the destruction of the two Republics. Great indeed is the proselytizing power of a press, especially when a number of apparently independent

---

refusal to give up the keys. Miss Walton replied, "Shoot me dead, then you can take the keys; not otherwise." In the end Miss Walton managed to send all the money and stamps away with Mr. Brussels, of Kenhardt, who arrived here yesterday.' 'Heroic Englishwoman! brutal Boers!' is the reader's comment. But the *Times* sub-editor had docked the tail of the Reuter telegram, which ran on as follows: 'And the rebels, admiring her pluck, left her alone, complimenting her on her courage.' The reader's comment is, 'Heroic Englishwoman! chivalrous Boers!' Those who would understand how the mind of the English people was prepared for going to war should peruse the telegrams sent by special correspondents of such newspapers as the *Times* and the *Daily News* in the spring and summer of 1899.

and usually conflicting organs are induced to coincide, or it is made worth their while to shed editors and to lose circulation in a given cause. 'They are like a battery,' cried Burke, 'in which the stroke of any one ball produces no great effect, but the amount of continual repetition is decisive. Let us suffer any person to tell us his story, morning and evening, but for one twelvemonth, and he will become our master.'

That there are other ways of manipulating the press than that of purchase is not disputed. Lord Palmerston was a past-master in the art of managing editors. In our own day Mr. Chamberlain's reputation stands high, especially as a contriver of spontaneous and contemporaneous outbursts of colonial opinion. An astonishing exposure of his method was provided by an indiscretion of the Melbourne correspondent of the *Times* during the battle between the Colonial Secretary and the Australian delegates over the appeal clauses of the Australian Federation Bill. The message ran as follows:

'Mr. Chamberlain has telegraphed to Sir. J. Madden, Acting Governor of Victoria, requesting him to collect and telegraph to him the opinions of the principal newspapers on the question of the proposed amendment to the Commonwealth Bill. The Melbourne daily papers are all willing to accept the amendment preserving the right of appeal to the Queen, and also favour the creation of an Imperial Appellate Court.'[1]

---

[1] See *Times*, May 5, 1900.

LIBERALISM AND THE EMPIRE

It is the first time that Downing Street has been actually caught working up the Colonial press against Colonial ministries.

The use of the press for the purposes of international finance, so strange to the average citizen that he is inclined to be incredulous, is no new portent to those who are versed in the *arcana imperii*. It is sixteen years since Mr. Gladstone, in reply to Sir Wilfrid Lawson's protest against war for Egyptian bondholders, admitted that foreign investors were as eager as our own jingoes to force Great Britain into a vast expenditure on Egypt.

'We are not willing,' he said, 'to be made the instruments of those who, for the sake of the millions sterling that have been invested in Egypt, are endeavouring, by every means they can employ, to bring the people of England blindfold into the assumption of immense responsibilities. . . . You may quote your foreign press, with every wire that governs the action of a portion of it pulled by those who are connected with this great pecuniary interest; it is not wonderful that they should act in this sense, because what could be more comfortable or satisfactory to them than that, having already profited largely by the intervention of England, they should secure by it fifteen or twenty millions more? What could be more satisfactory to them, there being no other consequence to be apprehended except the imposition of a terrific burden upon the people of England, and the undertaking of responsibilities of which I am certainly inclined to take a very serious measure?'[1]

Mr. Chamberlain and Mr. Rhodes are not, it may be surmised, troubled with conscientious scruples on this subject. That a great part of the press is, or may be, controlled by a group of financiers for bulling and bearing operations, that in smaller matters it can be turned this way or that by any Machiavelli who will cultivate it—these are not, in their view, diseases to be remedied, but facts to be weighed, forces to be used, and items to be calculated.

The same family likeness which appears on the face of their separate valuations of the press and of the Stock Exchange is also to be observed in the projects and propositions entertained by Mr. Rhodes and Mr. Chamberlain with regard to the commercial functions of a Government. Coincidences in the views of great contemporaries are always interesting, and especially so when any suspicion of collaboration is wafted away by an almost ostentatious air of detachment. It was in the summer of 1896 that Mr. Chamberlain developed Emporialism, and tried to storm the Congress of Chambers of Commerce with his notorious scheme of a Zollverein. Free Trade might seem to be an obstacle, but he adjured the delegates not to allow their minds to be fettered by

[1] Mr. Gladstone's speech, Hansard, April 3, 1884.

LIBERALISM AND THE EMPIRE

a 'pedantic adherence' to preconceived opinions. Mr. Chamberlain saw two fatal objections to the maintenance of Free Trade, each, of course, depending upon his own modest assumption that his own patent, 'the establishment of commercial union throughout the Empire, would not only be the first step, but the main step, the decisive step, towards the realization of the most inspiring idea that has ever entered into the minds of British statesmen.' Mr. Chamberlain's objections to Free Trade are, first, that it would offer no special or differential advantage to the trade of the Empire as such; second, that if we wait for the colonies to be converted to orthodoxy, we must postpone the hope of commercial union 'to the Greek Kalends.' Germs of 'the most inspiring idea' were found and welcomed by its patentee in a Resolution to be proposed by the Incorporated Board of Trade of Toronto, an 'essential condition' of which proved to be 'that Great Britain should consent to replace moderate duties upon certain articles which are of large production in the colonies.'

'Now, if I have rightly understood it, these articles would comprise corn, meat, wool and sugar, and perhaps other articles of enormous consumption in this country, which are at present largely produced in the colonies, and which might under such an arrangement be wholly produced in the colonies, and wholly produced by British labour. On the other hand, the colonies . . . would cease to place protective duties upon any product of British labour. That is the principle of the German Zollverein.'

It must be admitted that the Colonial Secretary contrived to put his proposal in a very alluring form when he enlarged upon the benefit of a union which would 'retain within the Empire and for the benefit of the Empire the trade now diverted to foreign lands.' But commercial men who were still actively engaged in trade, and had something to lose, looked at the proposal with dismay, and rejected it with alacrity. They saw that it meant the sacrifice of three-fourths of our trade for the sake of the remaining quarter—the loss of our biggest and richest customers for the sake of a slight improvement in commerce with distant colonies. Mr. Chamberlain thinks that a differential tariff (which would provide a practical incentive to the project of a continental coalition against England) would form the strongest bond of union for the British race. Those who have studied the history of English colonies and their relations with the mother-country know that those relations were never so strained as when the differential tariff system was in force. It was a tariff that lost us America, and all but lost us Canada. They recall Burke's philippics against the narrow views and little arts of those 'great statesmen' who believed regulation to be commerce, and imagined that teasing Custom-houses were the manufactories both of trade and of loyalty.

LIBERALISM AND THE EMPIRE

Foiled by the Chambers of Commerce, the Colonial Secretary's mischievous industry sought another outlet. In the days of the last Liberal Administration Mr. Rhodes had proposed the insertion of a further clause in the Charter, ' that the duty on *British* goods should not exceed the then Cape Tariff.' Sir William Harcourt replied that 'imported' must be substituted for 'British' in order to preserve our political policy of the Open Door and our economic policy of Free Trade. 'They fought,' said Mr. Rhodes, ' for the word *imported*, we fought for the word *British*.' ' We' were beaten, but in 1898 Mr. Rhodes was able to boast that the Chamberlain Administration had agreed to his clause. Meantime, added this egregious charlatan :

'The Cape tariff has come down to 9 per cent., and that practically keeps the trade of that new territory for ever for England. These 800,000 square miles will be purely British, and that will appeal to the people; and it is the people who rule. You thought a great deal of the unfairness of the French in putting on their protective tariff against us; but the French are perfectly right, and you have to learn the lesson if you are to keep your position.'

So we have to learn from Rhodesia the commercial value, not only of war and slavery, but also of protection. That Rhodesia has no trade, or none of which the Chartered Company will furnish accounts, that there are only about 10,000 mongrel whites in

IMPERIALISM AND FINANCE

this 'purely British' territory, and that we have no guarantee of the Cape tariff lasting for ever, are facts too small to trouble the mind or interfere with the rhetoric of 'the empire-builder.'

Let us, however, make the very large and generous supposition that this differential tariff in Rhodesia represents an additional annual trade for British producers of £10,000 a year, and an additional profit of £1,000. Let us forget entirely the responsibility of the Chartered Company for the Jameson Raid and the war, and forget also the heavy British investments in a company which has never paid a dividend. Assume that the profit goes on for ten years, and that in this way Great Britain nets a sum of £10,000. Now consider one single set-off. In the Chartered Company's report for 1898 the following passage may be read:

'Separate accounts are being kept of the amounts received and expended by the company in the discharge of its duties as a Government. These accounts comprise administrative revenue and expenditure and the cost incurred in the settlement of the country. The balance of expenditure under these headings not met by revenue will constitute a public debt whenever the inhabitants of Rhodesia are prepared to take over full responsibility for its administration. The Company will thus be reimbursed for a considerable portion of the outlay, and be left in possession of its mining and commercial interests.'

LIBERALISM AND THE EMPIRE

In the year 1898 their 'public debt' amounted, according to Lord Grey, to £10,000,000, according to Mr. Rhodes to £6,000,000. It is a clever device well worthy of its inventor. Observe the knowing smile with which the Board of Directors will welcome any serious item of chartered expenditure; see their wink at the secretary to order him to 'put that down to the debt account.' Who can doubt that if Mr. Chamberlain remains in power John Bull will take over this debt? So the British taxpayer must deduct at least £6,000,000 from the British manufacturers' profit of £10,000.

But trade follows the flag—follows it over jungles, swamps, deserts, through strait, rough, dense or rare; flies after it in the face of facts, arguments and arithmetic. Every Imperialist is at heart an Emporialist. Hunted by remorseless logic and indisputable facts out of all his snug corners, he will take refuge in this appeal to the purse. Expansion means commerce: trade follows the flag! A mountainous lie, and only to be removed by the exercise of a little common-sense.

'Figures prove,' wrote the late Lord Farrer, 'that the trade of the United Kingdom with foreign nations is three times as great as the trade of the United Kingdom with countries under the British flag, that this proportion has been substantially maintained during the last half-century—in fact, for the whole period for which we have trustworthy statistics.' In the quinquennial period 1855-59 the average annual trade with foreign countries was £209,000,000, that with British possessions was £76,000,000. In the period 1890-94 the figures were £477,000,000 and £166,000,000 respectively. Thus the foreign trade had risen in the second to 74·2, while the percentage which the trade with British possessions had borne to the total had altered from 26·7 to 25·8. Yet in the interval great stretches of territory had been annexed to the British Empire at enormous cost. A comparison of the two periods shows that in the second British exports to China, Russia and Holland trebled. Our exports to France rose from £3,000,000 in 1854 to £16,000,000 in 1890. The vast expenditure of British blood and British treasure upon Egypt has been singularly unproductive in those commercial harvests which Lord Salisbury's imagination painted in glowing colours. The average annual value of British exports to Egypt, which was £3,000,000 in 1880-84, had risen by painfully slow degrees to £3,500,000 in 1890-94. It is calculated that the British taxpayer has spent about £40,000,000 on Egypt and the Soudan. Never have desert lands been more thoroughly manured by more competent hands. But Lord Cromer sees no present prospect of the Soudan ceasing to be a drain upon the Egyptian Treasury. The same unremunerative expenditure of money, the same ruthless sacrifice of life, are going on in the malarious and tropical regions of East and West Africa. The Uganda railway, which was to have been completed for £3,000,000, is already estimated to cost £5,000,000. Our surpluses are thrown away upon the most worthless parts of the Empire.

But Mr. Chamberlain is unabashed. He 'believes confidently that this country benefits, and that it almost lives upon its colonial empire.'[1] He holds that we have a threefold duty: 'In the first place, to keep what rightly belongs to us; in the second place, to peg out claims for posterity; and in the third place, if anyone tries to rush these claims, gently to prevent them.'[2] Mr. Chamberlain is 'not afraid of expansion,' for he 'knows' that 'control over the markets is an absolute necessity, and that without it we could not possibly keep in comfort all the population which we have in these small islands.'[3] One would imagine from Mr. Chamberlain's speeches that the population starved until in 1895 he discovered the Empire, and began to take it in hand. Brummagem rhetoric cannot permanently prevail over common-sense. Business men know that trade follows not the flag, but the price-list and the quality of the article supplied. Human hecatombs are of no benefit to commerce. 'Murder for gain' is not a sound economic precept. Piracy was never a short-cut to national prosperity. 'We may be satisfied,'

[1] Hansard, August 2, 1898. [2] *Times*, January 18, 1898.
[3] *Times*, November 5, 1897.

wrote one of the wisest and most experienced of Mr. Cobden's disciples a year and a half ago, 'that to burden our people with the expense of seizing and governing unremunerative possessions, and with the cost of gigantic armaments created to defend such possessions from all possible rivals, will not tend to economic production; still less will it tend to economy if in the pursuit of new markets we are led into war with such countries as France, or Russia, or Germany.' Our Free Trade system is endangered by the very prosperity which it has evoked. Wealth has winked at swollen armaments, and revelled in spectacular demonstrations. Sham demagogues are blowing bubbles of military expansion, and the multitude watches, clapping its hands, certain that the short and costly splendour is inexpensive and eternal. The sons of the shrewd manufacturers who followed Cobden are sleeping partners in limited companies, and political supporters of Mr. Chamberlain. Their concerns are controlled by managing clerks. Useless in their industrial sleep, they are dangerous in their political dreams. They will wake up with a shock to find that the vulgar idols of Imperialism have ruined their fortunes without improving their stations. But it will not console a nation in a ditch to know that its leaders were blind impostors, and have fallen into it themselves.

LIBERALISM AND THE EMPIRE

III[1]

Those who in times of political drought watch anxiously the appearance of the horizon may have observed a cloud, at first small and local, now gathering volume, and spreading slowly but surely over the northern parts of this island. The movement to which this figure refers is complicated; its objects often appear to be incompatible; its supporters are sometimes involved in intestine dissensions; its divisions are so minute that they seem, if not parochial, at least beneath the notice of the great men who think in empires, while they move in metropolitan circles or revolve in cosmopolitan rings; and there is as yet a conspicuous want of that synthetic idealism which lifted the reformations of the thirties and forties from the base level of temporary expediencies, party manipulations, and the bare but comfortable necessaries of Cabinet existence. The movement is for a revision and reconstruction of local taxation. Its origin is not obscure.

Although the additional payments drawn from British taxpayers during the last few years may not

---

[1] Portions of the pages immediately following have appeared in the *Economic Journal* and the *Speaker*, to whose editors I am much obliged for permission to reprint certain passages.

have outstripped the increase of their wealth, they have been out of all proportion to the benefits actually derived. Secondly, the expenditure, though profligate upon injurious luxuries, fails lamentably to meet the rising standard of social needs and educational requirements. Thirdly, even supposing that the growing revenue had not been frittered away in endowment of classes, or in additions to unproductive and inefficient services, there would still remain in the minds of reformers a residuum of just discontent with the present incidence of local taxation. Fortunately our reformers, the *rari nantes*, may encourage themselves by observing the gradual diffusion in the public mind also of a vague dissatisfaction that growing needs are not met by growing revenues, and that the revenues themselves, improperly expended, are also improperly derived. No better evidence could be desired than the huge crop of resolutions passed by urban authorities in different parts of the kingdom during the last two or three years in connection with the subject of the rating of ground-values, or—to take another branch of municipal finance — the marked increase in the attempts made by municipalities to consolidate the areas and to acquire the collection of rates.[1]

[1] In this connection should be noted not only the private bill legislation of towns like St. Helens and Bradford, but also Sections 33, 34 of the Parish Councils Act, 1894, and Sections 10, 11 of the London Government Act, 1899.

LIBERALISM AND THE EMPIRE

In the sphere of Imperial finance the eye of criticism is turned rather to the expenditure, in that of municipal to the revenue. There prodigality calls for correction, here the framework of taxation. The upward movement of the revenue derived from rates is, indeed, parallel to that of the revenue derived from taxes; and in municipal politics there is almost always a party which fights (generally, but not invariably, under Tory colours) for what it calls economy. These people cannot understand that increased expenditure upon roads, drains, police, pleasure-grounds, and so forth, may, if honestly and judiciously applied, increase the wealth of a community. They do not see that in cutting down the salaries of their servants by a few hundreds they may easily produce, through blundering or corruption, a loss of as many thousands. Nothing can be worse for a democracy than to be governed, nothing better than to be served, by experts; but you must have a high salary to attract, and comfortable conditions to retain, the services of a first-rate specialist. As for the old communist contention that no one should have more than £300 a year, we may answer that it has also been contended that philosophers ought to be kings and kings philosophers. But weak human nature being what it is, and not what it ought to be, municipalities as well as individuals, when they want brain-work of a high order, must go into the market and bid for it.

IMPERIALISM AND FINANCE

True economy in municipal expenditure need not imply or involve reduction in revenue. A community which 'saves' in health and education stands to lose much health and more happiness. This is a very practical truth. Obvious as it seems, it is in one sense a new discovery; and a new discovery in politics generally brings a grievance with it. If people had remained content in the nineteenth century with the roads and drains of the eighteenth; if a few tottering veterans still served 'to keep the peace'; if a stream, a woman, and a pail still constituted a water-supply; if the sunset still brought darkness to the street and bedtime to the household, there would be no disturbing talk about the incidence of local taxation. But now every ratepayer in every town expects to have his street well lighted and paved. If he is not a Londoner, he expects those whom he elects to manage his municipal affairs to supply his home with a plentiful and perpetual current of gas and water at a low price. A proper system of drainage is a necessity; so is a town-hall; so, too, are parks, trams, bands. Libraries, technical schools, museums, wash-houses, and art-galleries are luxuries for which there is, happily, some demand. All these things involve rates, and when the demand-note, swollen by such items of expenditure, finds its way to the shopkeeper, already harassed by the poor-rate and the income-tax, to say nothing of other less sensible extortions, he feels the pinch, and cries out with pain. He is satisfied with the cake, and is ready that it should be larger; but he fancies that there are others who eat more and pay less. And he is right. Let us glance at the English law of rating. Of the two cardinal principles of taxation—the principle of ability and the principle of benefit—it may be laid down as an almost self-evident maxim that, while both are applicable to local as well as to imperial taxation, they are applicable in different degrees, according to the difference of the subject-matter. For imperial purposes ability, for local purposes benefit, should be the main criterion. So much will be admitted. The present Government, for example, has added some £20,000,000 annually to the imperial expenditure, but it would be quite impossible to apportion this according to benefit.

Municipal expenditure falls into a very different category. The maintenance of good waterworks, roads, drains, parks, and the like, by a local authority confers, no doubt, some benefit upon the whole country; but an overwhelming proportion of that benefit is absorbed temporarily by the occupiers, permanently by the owners, of property situated in the district. Unfortunately, the rating law of England is now, practically speaking, based upon the poor-rate. Rates are imposed upon visible immovable property within a given area. The assessment is upon the occupier. But his occupation must be 'beneficial.' But the criterion of rateability is not real but visible ability. The doctrine of the hypothetical tenant is very strictly applied, so strictly that the same hereditament will pay the same rate, whether it is occupied by a struggling farmer or a retired millionaire. Mr. Cannan, in his brilliant 'History of Local Rates,' notices that this characteristic feature of our system—which causes so much astonishment to our Continental critics—does, in fact, bring the principle of ability into contact with the principle of benefit. The compromise, slowly and clumsily evolved by justices of the peace, judges, and Parliaments, has, even to-day, one great practical merit. It avoids a local inquisition. In the spacious times of Elizabeth, when there were few towns, and fewer factories, when the well-to-do lived on their estates, and in a splendour proportioned to their rentals, visible ability approximated very closely to real ability; householding was an excellent basis for a rate which, like the poor-rate, is a national rather than a local concern. But the change in the habits of the rich, the growth of factories, the development of railways, the practical disappearance of the small freeholder, have revolutionized the rating question. So long as the wealthy classes are entirely composed of landed proprietors, and so long as your owners and occupiers are very largely identical, the principles of ability and benefit can be satisfied, if not logically and completely, at least easily and simultaneously, by rates with the same framework as the poor-rate; and it matters little whether the money so raised be applied to a national purpose, such as the relief of the poor, or to a local purpose, such as the provision of a drainage-system. In either case, your Elizabethan ratepayer is the proper person to pay rates. There he is able, here he benefits. But the twentieth century has shown a wide and widening divergence between the results which are to be obtained by applying our two principles. The distinct criteria of ability and benefit can no longer be harmonized in practice, and the situation has been made tolerable—or, rather, necessary and inevitable reformations are being postponed — only because palliatives have been applied in a variety of statutes.[1] For, even if the cost of making up a road or laying a sewer may be rightly apportioned, a heavy annual expenditure upon maintenance and repairs must always fall upon the General District Rate, which, under the present law, is imposed upon occupiers only.

[1] More especially by the device of apportionment, which enables a local authority to apportion expenses incurred in the *construction* of certain works among the adjoining 'owners' or lessors. (See Public Health Act, 1875, Section 4.) But the permanent benefit or 'melioration,' to use Pepys' word—accrues to the owners of the ground values, who do not necessarily, or as a rule, contribute as such to the preliminary expenditure, and never to the cost of maintenance.

IMPERIALISM AND FINANCE

Two imaginary cases will show the absurdity of the system. Suppose a doctor told two men (A and B, B being his own brother) that if they wanted to continue to live in good health they must each take a bottle of medicine a week, and that at the end of a year he sent in the whole bill of costs to A. The man pays unwittingly, and at first gratefully enough. But after a few years the health of both requires two bottles a week instead of one. A begins to find the bill very burdensome; he becomes restive and suspicious. The next step is to discover that his fellow-beneficiary is not a fellow-contributor, and the doctor is at last compelled to drop fraternity and divide the bill. The English Legislature, which has always been controlled by landlords, is the doctor. Local expenditure is the bottle of medicine. Rates are the bill. The occupier and the landlord are the two men who benefit. The occupier, whose comfort is increased, is called upon to pay the whole of the rates. The landlord, whose property is increased in value, has been let off scot-free by a sympathetic Legislature. Or, again, suppose that a local authority declined, and could not be compelled, to maintain its drains and its roads, then obviously everyone who could do so would remove from the district, and the rental would suffer a severe shrinkage. Probably there would be a short fit of keen economic bargaining, which would be concluded by a compact between landlords and tenants to divide

LIBERALISM AND THE EMPIRE

the costs of maintenance, though, of course, the actual proportion would depend upon the prosperity of the town and other local considerations.

In the second chapter of his fifth book, Adam Smith treats this subject with a force and earnestness that contrast with the timid tinkering spirit of some later writers. He deals with the inhabited house duty,[1] the taxation or rating of agricultural rents, and the taxation or rating of ground-rents, and regards the three with favourable eyes in an ascending order of merit; in the first he sees a natural graduation of an unobjectionable kind. But ground-rents and the ordinary rent of land are still more deserving of the attention of the Chancellor of the Exchequer, because, says Smith, they are 'a species of revenue which the owner enjoys without any care or attention of his own; though a part of the revenue should be taken from him in order to defray the expenses of the State, no discouragement will thereby be given to any sort of industry.' And he proceeds:

'Ground-rents seem in this respect a more proper subject of peculiar taxation than even the ordinary

[1] Mr. Jeeves, now the Town Clerk of Leeds, has suggested that the duty should be handed over to local authorities. This, no doubt, would be the proper course if it were retained. But had it not better be abolished, as it is a mere duplicate of rating? Why should the same man be taxed as well as rated in respect of his occupation of one and the same house?

IMPERIALISM AND FINANCE

rent of land. The ordinary rent of land is in many cases owing partly, at least, to the attention and good management of the landlord. A very heavy tax might discourage too much this attention and good management. Ground-rents, so far as they exceed the ordinary rent of land, are altogether owing to the good government of the Sovereign, which by protecting the industry either of the whole people, or of the inhabitants of some particular place, enables them to pay so much more than its real value for the ground which they build their houses upon, or to make to its owner so much more than compensation for the loss which he might sustain by this use of it. Nothing can be more reasonable than that a fund which owes its existence to the good government of the State should be taxed peculiarly, or should contribute something more than the greater part of other funds towards the support of that government.'[1]

Upon this masterly argument two remarks may be offered. The first is that our old-fashioned territorials who packed both Houses of Parliament took the opportunity, shortly after the publication of the 'Wealth of Nations,' to impose a tax upon the occupiers of inhabited houses, but that never in the direst straits of the Napoleonic wars did they

[1] Sceptics with a desire to be converted by modern statesmen and economists should read Mr. Asquith's recent speeches and certain brilliant contributions from the pens of Professors Marshall and Edgeworth to the Royal Commission on Local Taxation (C. 9528).

allow themselves to be driven to resort to the third-named source of revenue. The second remark is that if the reasons advanced by Adam Smith made a strong case for the imposition of a ground-tax in 1776, they make an overwhelming one for the imposition of a ground-rate in 1900. For if in Adam Smith's day a considerable proportion of national expenditure went indirectly to maintain or enhance ground values, a much larger proportion of local expenditure now produces directly the same effect.

One favourite argument often brought forward by the modern opponents of a rate upon ground values is that it would make no difference, because the owner of the ground would always be able to throw it upon the lessee. If such reasoning were honest, resistance would not be formidable; but we prefer to accept Professor Edgeworth's broad proposition that this tax tends to stick where it falls.[1] Adam Smith's opinion is also relevant: 'A tax upon ground-rents would not raise the rents of houses; it would fall upon the owner of the ground-rent, who acts always as a monopolist, and exacts the greatest rent which can be got for the use of the ground. . . . As the wealth of competitors would in no respect be increased by a tax upon ground-rents, they would probably not be disposed to pay more for the use of the ground.'

Smith adds, rather peremptorily, that unoccupied

[1] *Economic Journal*, 1897, 'Theory of Pure Taxation. I.'

houses ought not to be rated. But this is by no means clear, for if you rate on the English principle (expressly endorsed by Smith) your criterion is the rent at which they would let to the hypothetical tenant. There are many stupid, obstinate landlords, who over-estimate the value of their houses and keep them unlet for years. This is unprofitable for the landlord and prejudicial to the community. There are plenty of local Acts under which owners must pay rates on half the annual value of vacant houses, and thus a gentle financial pressure is applied to the short-sighted owner which is often good for him and always good for the community. But Smith's minor canon, whether right or wrong, did not apply to the ground-rate of an unoccupied house or of building land held against a market, and I do not doubt that he would have taken the side of Mr. Orford Smith against Sir Harry Poland in a recent controversy which may be found in one of the volumes of evidence given before the Royal Commission now for a long time sitting and incubating interim reports on Local Taxation. We may first consider Sir Harry Poland's abstract proposition:

'The principle is this: It [building land] is not land which is fit to be made a profit of by being let for the ordinary purposes of simple land; it is land of which at present no profitable use can be made, and which is waiting for the time to come when profitable use can be made of it by letting it out on a building contract.'

LIBERALISM AND THE EMPIRE

Therefore, says Sir Harry, building land ought not to be rated. But it would seem that even if future legislation is to be decided by past precedents, this distinguished pleader is battling for a precedent which is itself little better than an anomaly. For take the analogous case of agricultural land. 'It is quite clear,' said Lord Campbell in the case of Regina v. Fayle, 'that if a man who is in possession of the surface of the land, which in the ordinary use of it might be made productive, chooses only to grow thistles upon it for the use of the donkeys in the parish, he is nevertheless rateable in respect of the profit which it might reasonably be supposed he might make of it.' Our ancestors saw the policy of taxing those who allowed agricultural land to lie waste. Why not apply their wisdom to urban conditions? Sir Harry Poland was asked by one of the members of the Commission the following question:

'Supposing it to be proved to the rating authority that a man had some land close to a town, and we will say £800 had been offered to him for it, but that man persisted in standing out for £1,000 an acre, would you still say that that was unrateable land with the knowledge that it was land for which the man had been offered £800 an acre?'

Answer: 'I think it must be a question of degree. If he really believed it was worth £1,000 an acre, he had a perfect right to stand out for it.'

No one disputes the monopolist's right to 'stand

out' to any extent, but surely the monopolist has the less reason to complain of a law which would rate him on the basis of a lower value than that which he believed it to be worth. He might stand out for many years before his £1,000 would be rated away to £800. But the witness melted a little in the hands of Mr. Orford Smith, who put another case:

'Suppose you find in a town land fronting a street left a mere waste, while on either side of it and opposite to it you find land sold or let by the foot or the yard, would there be any difficulty in saying that that was building land?'

Answer: 'I think in that particular case you could say it was building land.'

Question: 'It must be a question of degree?'

Answer: 'Certainly. Of course, there may be difficulties in dealing with the property, and there may be some reason why it has not been let; for instance, the owner may say: "I think in all probability if I hold out longer I shall get a very much better price than that which has now been offered to me."'

Question: 'That is the case, no doubt; the question to my mind is whether it should not be rateable. Of course, the saleable value of adjoining land in such a case as that, or the ground-rent at which the land was let, would be a good guide to the value?'

Answer: 'Yes; a very good guide.'

Question: 'Although it might not be fair to rate a man at the full amount, he might fairly be rated for a considerable amount, having some regard to the value of the land—not by law, now, but I mean it would be a possible alteration of the law?'

Answer: 'He might possibly in that case, but you must not extend that principle too far.'

This little dialogue has been disinterred because it furnishes a concise illustration of the dialectical method of overcoming the best-equipped resistance to a real reform. The product of a ground-rate should be applied to the extinction of the more noxious forms of imperial doles, as well as to easing the burden of the occupier. In this way a Liberal Government will be able to reduce the income-tax to a reasonable figure. A ground-rate should be viewed, not as a substitute, but as an addition; for the occupier's rate is one of the most potent checks on municipal corruption, as the United States, which have it not, know to their cost. Every well-to-do working man ought to feel directly through the rates every rise and fall of municipal expenditure, just as he ought to feel directly through the income-tax every rise and fall of national expenditure. These are shadowy ideals difficult to realize; a patriotic statesman will guard jealously whatever substance they may be possessed of.

Another important topic that remains to be dealt with is suggested by the sentence already quoted from Adam Smith, in which he speaks of the owner of a ground-rent acting always as a monopolist.

IMPERIALISM AND FINANCE

So formulated, the proposition is too wide to be serviceable. It might lead to a practical argument of this kind :

> The supply of land is limited ;
> Therefore land is a natural monopoly ;
> Therefore land ought to be nationalized.

But this is only a syllogism of the Hegelian school of philosophers-turned-politicians. These gentlemen are apt to regard all distinctions as trifling, because they are only distinctions of degree. Fear of the commonplace is the beginning of much political error. It is true that natural local monopolies ought to be possessed or controlled by the local authority, for under such conditions alone can the public consumer be protected against exorbitant prices. We see that two competing sets of tram-lines cannot well run along one street. Accordingly, we rightly call tramways a natural monopoly, and treat them as a service in which strict public control or public ownership is eminently desirable. But land only falls under such a classification in rather exceptional places and circumstances.

Even building land in the centre of a large town rarely exhausts the full meaning of a *natural monopoly*. In Leeds, for example, which is parcelled out into comparatively small freeholds, you have the competition of sellers to set off against the competition of buyers; but there may very well be under our present laws an *artificial* local monopoly of land which will have an extraordinary effect upon prices. Fifteen miles from Leeds is a town of only a quarter the size under the ownership of a monopolist landlord, where house-rents are higher, not only relatively, but absolutely. 'We are deprived,' said a deputy from Huddersfield at a recent conference on the rating of ground values, 'of the healthy influence of competition between landowners in fixing the rents. The original estate was purchased in the Tudor period for less than £1,000. Now it is computed that the ground landlord (Sir John Ramsden) receives not less than £100,000 annually. The town has certainly been held back industrially by the position of affairs, and the work of the municipality has not been made any easier by the fact that they are practically in the hands of one ground landlord. The estate is being continually improved by public works and improvements made at the ratepayers' expense.'

These artificial land monopolies need not be municipalized or nationalized either by way of purchase or confiscation; they should be financially discouraged by a stiffly graduated rate which would induce everyone who is anything like a monopolist of property in a given rating area or union—and the boundary of every town union should be conterminous with that of the borough—to sell so much of it as would produce that 'healthy influence of competition' which Huddersfield and many other towns

IMPERIALISM AND FINANCE

vainly desire. If they refuse to sell, the difference between monopolistic and competitive rents will be returned automatically to the community.

Mr. Leonard Courtney has hinted in his reply to the questions of the Royal Commission on Local Taxation that if the same device of a progressive rate were applied to owners of agricultural land, 'there might be a tendency to break up large farms into smaller ones so as to escape the loss involved in letting farms of large size.'

If any doubt remain about the desirability of rating owners of land, I can imagine that it will take the form of an objection of this sort. 'Surely there must be some insuperable barrier of a practical kind that stands in the way of rating any person except the occupier. If not, why has it never been done?' I should be quite satisfied with the well-worn truth that English laws have been made by landlords. But there is a still better answer. Under the Advertising Stations (Rating) Act, 1889, owners of land in England may be and actually are at this very moment rated. There is no mystery about it. The thing is perfectly simple. You can put 'owner' just as well as 'occupier.' The Act does the deed in a delightfully English way. It says that the owner shall be 'deemed to be' occupier. Here are the very words of the Act (section 3):

'Where any land is used temporarily or permanently for the exhibition of advertisements . . . the person who shall permit the same to be used, or (if he cannot be ascertained) the owner thereof, shall be deemed to be in beneficial occupation of such land or part thereof, and shall be rateable in respect thereof to the relief of the poor and to all local rates, according to the value of such use as aforesaid.'

A hint towards the definition of ownership may be borrowed from the Small Dwellings Acquisition Act, the most puerile measure of the year 1899. According to the tenth section of that statute ownership shall be—

'Such interest or combination of interests in a house as, together with the interest of the purchaser of the ownership, will constitute either a fee simple in possession or a leasehold interest in possession of at least sixty years unexpired at the date of purchase.'

Under the Rating Act of 1874 the owner of a sporting right may be rated as an occupier, and a definition of owner for the purpose will be found in section 6 (4). So empty is the contention that ground-owners cannot be rated.

Finance is, as it were, the stomach of the country from which the other organs take their tone. A country with a corrupt Finance is not likely to be robust in its morality or vigorous in its policy—

'The soul grows clotted by contagion.'

It is often found that when a patient is suffering from complicated disorders the best way to restore health is to cure one, not that it can be said to be the cause of the rest, but rather that it is the principal centre of annoyance round which others congregate. The physician strikes at the centre and trusts that if his blow be successful the maladies which skirmish about will lose their violence and slacken their inroads upon the system. Now, if sound and honest Finance is a primary condition of political and social health, no department of national policy needs it more or gets it less than that which is concerned with the regulation of the traffic in alcoholic liquor. All modern economists and all modern economies have recognised in alcohol an essentially fiscal article. It is the peculiar misfortune of Great Britain that Chancellors of the Exchequer have never treated it as anything more. Our liquor legislators have kept their noses close upon the trail of revenue. They have never gone off on a false scent; in the ardour of pursuit they have seldom listened to any warning except the threats of the trade. To tax drink up to the point at which a decrease of consumption would balance the increase of duty has been the acme of statesmanship.[1] Morality's tribute is the decent tear that is allowed to trickle down the face of an

---

[1] Mr. Gladstone's reduction in the duty on light wines is a small exception. The sacred interests of the fisc were violated that the middle classes might be encouraged to cultivate a taste for a comparatively harmless form of alcohol.

LIBERALISM AND THE EMPIRE

unusually prosperous Budget in a year of abnormal drunkenness.

Now, bad as are the Liquor Laws, ill-considered Finance—in alliance with economic tendencies—is rapidly making them worse. The License System in England is the laughing-stock of the world. It is an accepted principle that a Government ought not to confer a valuable franchise upon an individual, except for an adequate consideration. Patents and copyrights are the stimulus as well as the reward of invention. They confer a strictly limited monopoly. They are the exceptions which prove the principle. But what words can adequately describe the folly and enormity of a law by which there are given annually throughout this kingdom, to individuals arbitrarily chosen, by authorities arbitrarily appointed, thousands of lucrative franchises to which the donees have no claim, and for which they make a nominal payment only? If a town council were to hand over the franchise of its streets for nothing to a tramway company, its action would be regarded as a qualification for the lunatic asylum; and yet in every town and county franchises certainly far more valuable in the aggregate are presented every year to the retailers of alcoholic liquor. These licenses are neither more nor less than monopolies; for if they were granted freely to all applicants their value would dwindle away. One single example must suffice. In a small northern town a new license was granted in 1897 to a small house valued at £3,500. On receipt of the license the owner promptly sold the house for £24,500. Thus the small northern town lost a sum of £21,000 by a single transaction.[1] There are few people who realize that the patronage of the justices of the peace in this country is worth infinitely more than that of the Lord Chancellor and all the Ministers of the Crown put together, and that if sale were substituted for patronage poor-rates in some localities would be entirely abolished, and a large sum remain over for other municipal purposes. Luckily, the fact that there is an annual distribution of patronage does not prove that it must go on for ever. English law declines to distinguish between the grant and the renewal of a license. 'A new license is a renewal,' said Lord Bramwell, 'as we talk of a new lease being a renewal.' Our Supreme Court, the House of Lords, in the case of Sharp v. Wakefield (1891 A.C., 173), decided once for all, in complete accordance with the principles of common law and common-sense, that the justices have absolute discretion[2] to refuse a renewal as well as a new application.

So far attention has been directed to one aspect

[1] See for many other typical instances 'The Temperance Problem,' Rowntree and Sherwell (2nd ed.), pp. 337-346.

[2] *E.g.*, misconduct need not be alleged. It is enough if the justices think that the house is unnecessary for the neighbourhood. No compensation is to be given.

only of the public-house monopoly. But monopoly breeds monopoly, and the detached local monopolies established by statute have been supplemented very rapidly in the last half-century by more or less secret combinations. A new map of England is required, showing first the houses licensed to sell liquor; secondly, the breweries and distilleries; and thirdly, the licensed houses which are 'tied'—that is to say, under the control of a particular brewery or distillery, and compelled to sell its liquor only. Only a small percentage of public-houses are now owned by the licensee. The amalgamation of breweries and brewery companies is putting the control of the trade and of its policy into fewer and fewer hands, until the liquor monopoly threatens to dominate Great Britain as completely as De Beers dominates South Africa. This change in the configuration of the trade demands a change in its laws. A development and unification of monopoly into an organized and centralized system may be a source of weakness as well as of strength; the ripening processes may end in decay and dissolution. The legislator has only one rope to cut when a whole trade is tied together.

The cause of temperance reform made a great advance when Sir Henry Campbell-Bannerman adopted Lord Peel's minority-report as a basis for practical legislation. In spite of the war fever, a knowledge of the political and social menace is being slowly diffused. The connection of intemperance with crime and lunacy is forcing itself upon the general intelligence. People are aware of a recent increase in the amount of drink consumed per head of the population, and of a parallel increase in the proportions of lunacy. Inebriety is the middle term, and there are distinct signs, both administrative and legislative, that the treatment of inebriates is engaging more and more of the public attention.

No one supposes that the payment of an adequate price by the licensee would conduce to the traffic being carried on in a less moral and public-spirited way than at present. Nor does any part of the financial reform just indicated contain the prime demerit of novelty. The local character of licenses is already recognised. In 1835, Lord John Russell proposed to transfer the patronage from the justices of the peace to town councils. In 1871, Mr. Bruce's Licensing Bill, brought forward on behalf of the Government of the day, and providing for a ten years' notice and no compensation to existing licensees, contained the following clause :

'Where a new publican's general certificate is to be granted for any licensing district, the same shall be granted to the person who offers by tender to pay for the same during the continuance of the certificate the highest annual percentage on the annual value of his premises.'

If the Bill of 1871 had passed, and the proceeds

of the licenses had been devoted to local purposes, less would be heard of the intolerable burden of rates.

The table of license duties now in force is not merely unjust and anomalous, it offends common-sense. If the annual value of the licensed house is under £10, the duty is £4 10s., or 45 per cent.

Annual Value.			Duty.	Percentage.
£10	to	£15	£6	40
15	,,	20	8	40
20	,,	25	11	44
25	,,	30	14	46
30	,,	40	17	42½
40	,,	50	20	40
50	,,	100	25	25
100	,,	200	30	15
200	,,	300	35	11½
300	,,	400	40	10
400	,,	500	45	9
500	,,	600	50	8
600	,,	700	55	7¼
700 or more			60	—

The richer the house, the less the license duty. Financial laws are turned upside down for the liquor traffic. Exactions from the poor, abatements for the rich. Licensed victuallers live in a looking-glass world of their own.

It may be objected that a revision of the law would be unfair to genuine hotels, but we turn to 43 and 44 Vict., c. 20, sec. 43 (4), and find that their case has been already provided for with the most extravagant generosity :

'Where in the case of premises of the value of fifty pounds or upwards it shall be proved to the satisfaction of the Commissioners that the premises are structurally adapted for use as an inn or hotel for the reception of guests and travellers desirous of dwelling therein, and are mainly so used, the amount of duty to be paid on a license to retail spirits shall not exceed twenty pounds.'

So much of the fiscal aspects of our liquor monopoly; and with these partial hints at the nature of the evil and its remedies, I must bring my brief examination of some present problems of local finance to a close.

'Economists' of the jingo and protectionist school shake their heads solemnly over the increase of local expenditure, and tell the people that the only possible means of providing more revenue is by resorting to *octrois*, or to imperial doles provided out of a protective tariff. They seek to lessen small ills by instituting great ones. There are two opposite dangers which the democracy has to avoid in its municipal policy. It may fall on its back into a corrupt slush of monopolies or face foremost upon the hard asphalt of bureaucratic collectivism. Either mishap may be avoided by a wise and strenuous Liberalism.

LIBERALISM AND THE EMPIRE

IV

Now that some indication has been given, not only of the financial and political dangers which are to be apprehended from the growing power of speculative finance and the growing lust of territorial aggrandizement, but also of the pressing grievances suffered by the middle classes under the present law of rating, it would have been natural and proper to draw the whole complex subject together by a survey of the existing relations between local and Imperial finance, and by a contrast of the relations which exist with those which ought, under an amended system, to be substituted.

But this is no occasion for vulgarizing the mysteries of Probate or Excise. The whirlwind of war whips these important trifles into obscure corners where they must rest until the stir is over or a spell of bad trade brings on a fit of public economy. Then the national accounts will be overhauled, and a *lucidus ordo* will reign again over a system muddled by the doles and allowances of Tory finance. It is no time to patch up small leakages when one huge wave threatens to swamp the ship. A barbarous war, that has laid bare the very foundations of society in South Africa, is returning against the bulwarks of the British Constitution. Let us prepare ourselves for the danger by trying once again to take

IMPERIALISM AND FINANCE

the measure of its offensive strength and the means of resistance which are available.

In his Budget, brought forward on March 5, 1900, Sir Michael Hicks-Beach estimated expenditure for the coming financial year at the unparalleled sum of 155 millions, which exceeded by 43 millions his estimate for the previous year, and exhibited a deficit on the existing basis of taxation of about 38 millions of money. The estimates for the army and navy were just under 30 millions apiece, and to this 60 millions 31 have to be added (if we accept the modest reckoning of officials) for the cost of the war from March 31 to September 30, 1900.

When the army and navy estimates were introduced, the *Times* ordered the House of Commons to be 'prompt and acquiescent,' and to display 'no considerations of economy.' But when, on the night of the Budget, this great newspaper realized that a small fraction of the deficit was to be provided for by an increase of the income-tax, it discovered that an addition to the National Debt ' has a moral value which can never attach to mere payment of taxation.' Nay, ' a war-loan offers an opportunity for the country to show what is the depth and reality of its patriotic enthusiasm at a moment of national trial.'[1]

But though the *Times* and its backers preferred a

[1] *Times*, March 6, 1900. The 'khaki loan' patriotism was a success. Many of the allottees resold immediately at a profit. On June 1 the loan stood at 2 premium.

LIBERALISM AND THE EMPIRE

loan to direct taxation, it had a pet scheme of its own for securing a vast increase of revenue by a complete change of fiscal policy. It was not (in justice we must admit) wholly in favour of that borrowing policy which Mr. Disraeli in his younger days stigmatized as Dutch finance.

At the beginning of the year 1899, the *Times* had opened its columns to an 'expert of high authority.' The idea of this great newspaper, which has since been so busily engaged in disturbing the *Pax* and distributing the *Encyclopædia Britannica*, seems to have been that our system of taxation suffers from three fatal evils :

1. It is too simple.

2. It is too Free-Tradish (if the adjective be permissible).

3. It bears too heavily upon the rich man (especially if he owns land), and extracts too little from the pockets of the labouring classes.

A financier armed with three propositions the exact converse of these would, it is submitted, be well, though not adequately, equipped for the office of Chancellor of the Exchequer. Yet it was whispered about that this 'expert' is a man of vast official experience.

Had he confined himself to abstractions, had he been content to preach in the monastic seclusion of a college or in the unruffled atmosphere of the British Association, his fallacies might well have been left to the lethal processes of the lecture-room. Unfortunately, he seized the psychological moment, and entered the world through the *Times*; he may even claim to have impressed the Tory party, and to have influenced the Budget of 1899, though his advice was rejected in the Budget of 1900. Let us, therefore, treat him with respectful curiosity as an authoritative herald of Tory finance.

The first point that struck the imagination was his alarm—not for the Submerged Tenth, not at the neglect of the aged and deserving poor, not at the increase of inebriates and lunatics, not at the rise in the poor-rate. No; all his concern was for the capitalist, whose laborious and patriotic accumulations were being overtaxed by his own creatures, the Government of the day. In order to set things right, the Death Duties must be thoroughly overhauled, and the income-tax 'instantly' reduced by 'at least twopence.' The deficiency thus increased should be met by the imposition of a duty of a halfpenny a pound upon sugar and of a shilling a quarter upon wheat. So modest a revival of Protection was intended to be a prelude which should set the popular affections upon the attainment of a wider scheme and elevate into a practical canon the following proposition: 'The greater the variety of the indirect taxes, the more likely they are in the aggregate, if they are at all moderate, to press evenly upon the resources of the community.'

LIBERALISM AND THE EMPIRE

There is something very ingenious about the theory of even pressure. It is admitted that the poor man consumes more flour, it is probable that he consumes more sugar, than the rich; but let us assume that their consumption is only equal, and what follows? Why, simply this: that in the opinion of 'an expert of high authority' the most equitable system of taxation, and that to which we should now gradually approximate, is one in which all citizens will pay alike, without reference to their abilities or incomes: so that if our expert were reduced to a single source of income, he would select the poll tax or a duty on corn.

The fallacy that the best and fairest system is that which presents a great variety of smallish taxes was promulgated by Arthur Young. The theory was exploded by Adam Smith; but the creature lived and flourished in the wretched era of Pittite finance. Killed by Hutchison, it was buried by Peel. Exhumed by Sir George Cornewall Lewis, it was reinterred with much solemnity by Mr. Gladstone. It reappeared, as we have seen, in the year following his death, under the patronage of the *Times* newspaper.

The Budget of 1899, and still more Sir Michael's Budget speech, showed traces of these antiquarian doctrines, and the revivalist was encouraged to make another effort in the spring of 1900. 'In some letters before and at the time of the last

IMPERIALISM AND FINANCE

Budget'—to quote the remarkable article which appeared from the same pen in the *Times*, March 5, 1900—'I gave reasons for the view that the time had come for a thorough revision of our financial methods.' Since then a serious war had arisen, 'one of those very contingencies which made a revision of our financial system imperative.' Of the increased expenditure due to the war, he believed that at least ten millions represented a permanent annual addition to the military expenditure of the year preceding the war. The editor of the *Times* was in full agreement with his expert:

'Apart from direct war expenditure, we have in sight a continuing extra expenditure of apparently at least some ten millions of money per annum. It is made up of what is called a normal increase of the army and navy estimates—say a couple of millions, another couple of millions due to projected additions to the army, and six millions for "temporary" measures of home defence.'

But the prophetic vision of the expert saw far beyond the figures of the Budget before him:

'I venture to doubt whether the permanent increase of our defence expenditure will not be found a year or two hence to be more than double this sum. The charge imposed by the war amounts, in fact, to this, that instead of having at home an army of about 100,000 nominally, we ought at least to have 250,000, about 100,000 of whom would be recruits under training.'

LIBERALISM AND THE EMPIRE

These additions would of course have to be composed of the most expensive arms—mounted infantry, cavalry, and artillery. However much estimates are cut down, '£20,000,000 will be absolutely required. . . . The £10,000,000 which appears to be the idea of the Government in the estimates is in any case obviously inadequate.'

As we are calculating whether another shilling added to the income tax will yield this 'inevitable' addition to our 'obviously inadequate' expenditure, and as we are trying to estimate the loss which will fall on the nation through these 150,000 men (earning, say, £150,000 a week) being withdrawn from the ranks of the wealth-producers into the army of the wealth-destroyers, we find ourselves hurried by our financial guide into an entrancing plan whereby the required sum will be picked from the taxpayer's pocket almost unknown to the taxpayer. He will be puzzled to know how his means became suddenly so pinched and straitened. 'Sugar,' we read, being 'an article of general luxury and common consumption,' is 'obviously a most suitable article for the purpose.' It is true—as visions of decaying manufacturers of jam, cocoa, or confectionery cross the expert mind—that a duty on sugar 'will involve some interference unfortunately with a considerable trade; but when we balance advantages and disadvantages, it is evident that sugar is one of the most convenient articles to touch when a great deal of revenue has to be raised.' A duty of £10 a ton or a penny a pound would bring in about £12,000,000 sterling. The second article upon which duties should be levied is foreign corn. We are advised to proceed gingerly at first with an imposition of a shilling per quarter, which will bring in two millions. A third addition (of three or four millions in the first place) should be drawn from duties upon other agricultural produce imported from abroad :

'In proposing such duties, however, we are evidently on more dangerous ground than in the case of sugar. The sentiment against taxing the food of the people is almost certain to be worked upon by politicians. The outcry will no doubt be raised also that such taxes are contrary to Free Trade.'

The reply to such fanciful objections is that the money must be raised. The breach of Free Trade is only 'technical ;' *de minimis non curat lex*; anything is better than direct taxation. Let none indulge in 'nice statistical calculations.' This is no time for argument or reason. 'When our city is burning, we must put out our fire the quickest way we can.'

When a fiery summons to pull down that commercial fabric which has been jointed together by the skilful workmanship of our wisest statesmen is issued with the authority of the *Times* at its back, when that same powerful newspaper, which smiled upon the emancipation of our commerce, cries out that 'indirect taxation rests upon an absurdly narrow basis,' and denounces 'the slavish deference of successive Governments to the childish clap-trap about a free breakfast-table,'[1] it may be taken for granted that a dangerously strong body of opinion is growing up in the Unionist party which is determined to aggravate the late sensational increases of military expenditure, and will be only too glad if the pressure of taxation perverts our governing classes from Free Trade, and so revives the old predominance of territorials over manufacturers. What is mere loss of trade compared with a restoration to power of a landed aristocracy?

It may be well that the country should for a season writhe under the growing weight of an unnecessary burden. Let us wilfully close our eyes to the strip of silver sea, and we shall perhaps understand before it is too late what regimental despotism and grinding poverty attend the creation of a Continental army and the erection of a protectionist tariff. Our Chancellor of the Exchequer has allowed the estimates for naval, military, and civil services to rise in five years from sixty-nine to ninety millions. The calculation, which is his own, excludes the war and does not err on the side of exaggeration. He knows very well that a great effort will be made by Army Leagues and Navy Leagues to secure the enormous additions demanded by newspapers like the *Times*,

[1] *Times*, March 5, 1900.

IMPERIALISM AND FINANCE

and that in particular 'there will be a demand in certain quarters for a great increase in our regular army.'[1] He reminded his constituents of 'wise words' used by Mr. Disraeli at the end of the Crimean War, when that statesman moved, with the concurrence and support of Lord John Russell and Mr. Gladstone, that the cost, though not the efficiency, of our military and naval establishments should be put back to the level of 1853. The present writer will not be open to the reproach of 'Little Englandism' if he recalls a Disraelite statement of that policy which the Chancellor of the Exchequer now implores his own party to 'imitate':

'" It would be most unwise for the country to allow itself to suppose that it could guard itself against the recurrence of many mortifying incidents which occurred at the commencement of the war by habitually supporting a much larger military establishment than is necessary for the ordinary interests of the country," and to expend in this way "resources which, having been accumulated by a wise system of economy, have enabled us to meet our difficulties with so much comparative ease." He went on: "There is a great difference between an effective and an expensive army. We may have a military system which is perfect, and which at the same time is founded on a wise economy. The

[1] Speech at Bristol, May 16, 1900. 'I disbelieve,' he said, 'in the necessity for any such increase.' The speech was ignored by the Unionist press.

military establishment which we sanction should be a model, rather than a force adequate to any great occasion which may hereafter arise."'

The fact that Mr. Disraeli went so far as this in 1858, and actually moved a resolution in favour of economy (to the great embarrassment of Lord Palmerston), derives additional significance from the circumstances of the Crimean War. Serious as the blunders of the War Office and the delinquencies of the contractors have proved in the South African campaign, there has been nothing to compare with that complete breakdown of military organization which disgraced the earlier stages of the Crimean War. The new harum-scarum Imperialism has not one-fifth of the excuses of Palmerstonianism, yet its panic-notes are thrice as treble and its proposals are three times more costly.[1] Nor is it probable that statesmen of the calibre of Mr. Gladstone, Mr. Disraeli, and Lord John Russell can be counted upon to stand for a wise economy in the Parliament of 1901.

For the moment there is no sign of a reaction. So long as the theatre is open and the drama proceeding you cannot expect the audience to turn away its eyes from the stage. Yet the time cannot be far distant when a cry for retrenchment will excite loud

[1] In 1858 Lord Palmerston was content with a new level of military and naval expenditure, only seven millions above that of 1853.

IMPERIALISM AND FINANCE

and responsive echoes in the country. A shilling income-tax is a thought-compelling institution even in a year of prosperity. It is an institution likely to involve its founders in much unpopularity when the remorseless cycle of trade brings round another period of small profits and low wages. So long as Peel and Cobden and Gladstone flourished, the manufacturing classes generally stood by the policy of peace, Free Trade, and retrenchment, which had made their fortunes. A new generation has grown up of men whom ignorance and negligence of public affairs combined with aspirations after 'smart society' has driven into the party of privilege and economic reaction. Property is preparing against itself forces which, wisely handled, may not only rehabilitate the Liberal party, but greatly improve the State. Vast fortunes accumulated by monopoly and stock-jobbing arouse hatred, malice and disgust. Riches so acquired are seldom usefully employed, and indeed it is very difficult for a millionaire, however honest, to get rid of his income without injury to the commonwealth. Graduation of the income-tax appears to be dictated to our people not only by the costliness of good public education and of other services which are needed if England is ever to realize even faintly that far-off ideal of equality of opportunity, but also by the plain rule of self-defence. Democratic as it may appear on paper, the British Constitution is very little better than a pretence. It is only a mask over the face of plutocracy. How can a poor man, *preserving his independence*, enter the House of Commons? How can a poor man, *preserving his independence*, write for the press? If it be true that these two avenues are practically barred to those who refuse to crawl or have not enough to ride, then the government of Great Britain must be called a plutocracy—a rule of rich men and their instruments. With regard to the press, which has been called the Fourth Estate of the realm, all hope of improvement rests upon the prospect of co-operation between wealth and intellectual honesty. The whole staff of a journal should share in its ownership, and those who write should exercise control over its policy. There is a good demand for honesty; the deficiency is in its supply. The remedy is to be found in a recognition of the need for radical changes in a corrupt system.

A remedy for the other evil must be sought in political finance. The payment of election expenses, an old plank in the *platform* of the Liberal party, will assist in removing the barrier which monopolistic wealth interposes between public spirit and public service. But the temptations and degradations to which aspiring indigence is exposed can only be removed by payment of members, a reform which should be accompanied by a strict provision that no Member of the House of Commons shall be the director of more than one public company. Mr.

IMPERIALISM AND FINANCE

Gladstone made it a rule that Ministers should not hold directorships in public companies, but the usage has been so grossly violated by Members of Lord Salisbury's Administration (which has contained more directors than Ministers) that it ought surely to receive the approval of Parliament and the sanction of law. If salaries of £5,000 a year are not enough to enable Ministers to compete with the ambitious poverty of West-End life, let them be increased. Of all those compromises, reconciliations, and accommodations which offend and impair public morality, the Rhodesian — between business and politics, between Board meetings and Cabinets—is the worst. We all know how insidious are the ways of corruption, how unconsciously motives of private gain may work upon virtuous resolves. Stringent, then, is the duty imposed upon men in office to live and move in a clear air far above the atmosphere of suspicion.

One danger can hardly be escaped. The Stock Exchange, acting upon the Company Laws, has placed the ownership of industry and the means of distribution and production upon a basis that is very largely speculative, with results that are often disastrous to the public interest. Take the case of the liquor laws. Is not the enthusiasm of the reformer too often damped by the dividends of the investor? Take the still blacker case of South African Companies, in which the governing classes of this country had invested so largely. The consciences of these investors are far too easy. Messrs. Rhodes, Beit, Albu, Goerz, and the rest stand between them and their victims. The opulence of Park Lane is squeezed from the compound. The geese that lay golden eggs for London society are of a migratory habit, and possess a power Hans Andersen might have envied of changing their plumage and their form. For these ingenuous auriferous geese that waddle through the vulgarized drawing-rooms of London and Parisian seasons are vultures when they flap their wings and sharpen their talons over Kimberley, Johannesburg, and Rhodesia. In nineteenth-century Africa, as in eighteenth-century India, 'all the vices operate by which sudden fortune is acquired.' Arrived in England, the exploiters of compulsory labour and the instigators of civil war ' will find the best company in this nation at a board of elegance and hospitality.'

'They marry into your families; they enter into your senate; they ease your estates by loans; they raise their value by demand; they cherish and protect your relations which lie heavy upon your patronage; and there is scarcely a house in the kingdom that does not feel some concern and interest that makes all reform of our African Government appear officious and disgusting, and, on the whole, a most discouraging attempt. In such an attempt you hurt those who are able to return kindness or to resent injury. If you succeed you save those who cannot so much as give you thanks.'[1]

If the theory that the Liberal party depends upon the subscriptions of a few magnates be a true theory, then another party must and will be formed. But if its strength, as we rather suspect, lies in moral enthusiasm, it will not be deterred by plutocratic and aristocratic considerations from a grand remonstrance. It will admit that African like Indian government is likely for a long time to be 'in its best state a grievance.' It will see the difficulties of reform, but it will see its necessity too. Agreeing with Burke that 'it is an arduous thing to plead against abuses of a power which originates from our own country, and affects those whom we are used to consider as strangers,' we shall agree also that 'the correctives should be uncommonly vigorous, and the work of men sanguine, warm, and even impassioned in the cause.'

[1] See Burke's speech on Fox's East India Bill, December 1, 1783. I have ventured to substitute the word 'African' for the 'Eastern' of the original.

THE EXPLOITATION OF INFERIOR RACES IN ANCIENT AND MODERN TIMES:

AN IMPERIAL LABOUR QUESTION WITH A HISTORICAL PARALLEL.

THIS essay is an attempt in a purely scientific spirit, without controversial animus and without sentiment, to throw a little side-light upon a vast problem of the present and future by the study of a very similar problem, and a great failure to solve it, in the past. It proposes no detailed remedies for the evils with which it deals, but merely attempts to put in a fairer and perhaps a more philosophic light a subject which is wrapped in a glow of vainglory for the majority of English people, and is apt to be scouted with unpractical aversion by the more generous.

The labour question for any community is, in the first place, the question how that community is to get its work done, what is the most effective method, the cheapest method. In common parlance, of course, the phrase is understood in the special and partial

EXPLOITATION OF INFERIOR RACES

sense: 'What are the right conditions of life for the labouring classes?' that being the particular side of the question which interests men most at the present moment. But the first and stricter meaning really includes the second. If the community gets its work done in the best way, the condition of the workers must be right; for work that seems to be cheap must in the end be ruinously dear if part of the price paid for it is the degradation, moral or physical, of the workmen. And, on the other hand, if any supposed improvement in the workers' condition really means that the community is being ill served or paying dear for bad work, the improvement must necessarily be both transient and unreal.

Our Imperial labour problem, then, is this: How is the British Empire in the twentieth century to get its work done? The conditions are:

First, that we have an enormously complex society, based upon intricate and highly-developed systems of manufacture and commerce, involving every degree of brain and manual work from the highest to the lowest—a society which depends for its existence on its inventors, its engineers, its organizers, its craftsmen with specially trained powers of eye and touch, just as much as it depends upon its masses of labourers, skilled and unskilled, who by strength or patience or discipline or mere docility, can make themselves in some way useful to the commonweal.

In the second place, it is a society made up of a

LIBERALISM AND THE EMPIRE

vast number of races, so profoundly diverse that the supposed racial differences of English, Scotch, and Irish, or even of German and French, are almost unnoticeable by comparison; the numerous tribes of Africa, from Kruboys to Hottentots, all with different aptitudes, and capable, in different degrees, of education; the races of India, interminably various, from the subtle intelligence of the Parsee, Mahratta, and Bengali to the mere wildness of Bhils and Khonds;[1] the obedient strength of the Bombay Kuli and the Lascar; the cheery vigour of Burmese and Malay; the adroit and patient docility of the Chinaman. There is no need to particularize further; we have as our fellow-subjects an immense number of different breeds of men, each doubtless possessing its own powers and qualities.

If we add the third obvious condition, great and increasing facilities of transport, it becomes obvious, in general terms, what the answer to our problem is likely to be. It is only the due deduction from the old doctrine of Free Trade—that countries ought to produce what they are best fitted to produce, and allow the industries for which they are not fitted to seek for more suitable soil elsewhere. Society will presumably use negro labour, or Chinese labour, or Hindoo labour where it is better at the price than

[1] The Bhils, since these words were written, are said to have been practically exterminated by famine—one solution of the question.

EXPLOITATION OF INFERIOR RACES

British labour, just as it uses American wheat or German lead-pencils.

Such being in the most general terms the probable answer to our modern labour question, we may postpone for the moment any consideration of how far it is desirable or how far it is likely to be modified, and turn at once to the historical parallel.

One of the commonest remarks to be found in any treatise on ancient history is the antithesis that ancient society was founded on the institution of slavery, modern society on free contract. This generalization is, of course, roughly true, but it needs great modification in both its branches.

What is a slave? Historically speaking, a slave is essentially an alien, a foreigner, who, in the midst of a community where everyone else has his regular status and definite rights, has no rights and no status. The Latin word *servus* means, of course, a man saved, *i.e.*, an enemy taken in war, whom you have a right to kill, but whom you prefer to make work for you. Our own word 'slave,' like the now obsolete 'nigger,'[1] denotes merely a particular race of men. A slave is a Slav prisoner of war, such as were sold in thousands over Europe during the great wars of the Saxons and Franks against the Slavs from the ninth to the twelfth century.

A Slave, then, is an Alien, and the most primitive

[1] The word 'nigger' is still used by South Africans very much in the old sense. Naturally.

LIBERALISM AND THE EMPIRE

ancient communities admitted no aliens. The earliest Greek, Roman, and Semitic societies that we know, so far from being based on slavery, only know of the slave as an accidental product of war possessed by the wealthy heads of families. The slaves are almost all female, and slavery practically exists for the sake of polygamy, which has always been a rare and expensive luxury for the few. In the second place, if we take those periods of history in which slavery was really a cardinal fact in the social structure, and the trade in slaves became one of the necessities of commerce, even then, it is worth while suggesting, the essential character of the thing demanded and the thing supplied by that trade did not lie in the legal fact of slavery. The essence of the demand was not legal, but economical; the commerce of the time demanded cheap, submissive, and 'fully exploitable' labour, and this was supplied in the shape of captive or destitute aliens.

A free patriarchal society, with several ranks and grades, but with no slavery—that is the general type presented by most of the earliest communities that we find in Greece, Italy, and Asia Minor. But there is one great fact which prevents it being universal. Some communities, even in the remotest times known to us, already consist of Colonists—that is, of invaders occupying a territory which formerly belonged to another race, and holding that other race in subjection. When the earliest Greek adven-

EXPLOITATION OF INFERIOR RACES

turers first set foot in Sicily, in North Africa, in Asia Minor, and on the shores of the Black Sea, they followed in the main exactly the same path of action that has been trodden by all other colonists since. They first fought and beat the natives, then more or less vigorously, for longer or shorter periods, they proceeded to exterminate them like wild beasts or vermin. They ended in most cases by allowing them to settle down into some condition of subjection in which their lives were safe, and in which very often they tended to be joined and reinforced by broken men—criminals, bankrupts, and exiles—of the race of the rulers. There were many varieties of condition. A Helot was attached to a particular master;[1] a Jebusite was attached to a community; Penestæ, Bithynians, natives of Sicily, and others, all lived in various degrees of distress or prosperity, slavery or freedom. But they were all subject races. This particular social condition, the presence of a superior in the territory of an inferior, is the most fruitful germ, it is almost the very origin and explanation, of slavery. And we must bear it in mind as a potent factor while we now turn to consider how in the free societies of Greece proper the slave trade in the strict sense of the word reached such immense proportions.

[1] The old Helots, it may be observed in passing, were a primitive agricultural community, dispossessed and held down by an invasion of conquering Outlanders. Sir A. Milner seems to have misunderstood the meaning of the word.

LIBERALISM AND THE EMPIRE

Most of the Greek States about the eighth or seventh century B.C. were emerging from a state of society very like that of the Middle Ages—an unprogressive, uncommercial society, with the chief power in the hands of noble families who owned the land. Such trade as there was was carried on by barter; religious bodies were very strong; foreigners seldom seen, and when seen usually robbed. But during the next two centuries a great movement took place, which resulted in changing those quiet, semi-barbarous mediæval communities into the great Greece of the fifth century, the society which in so many ways has left its indelible stamp upon the world, and in some ways perhaps reached the high-water mark of human attainment. We are concerned only with the economic change; from being mediæval, Greek society—not in all States, of course, but in those which were open to the movement—became modern.

Let us mention in passing the merest heads of the development. There was great pressure of population at home, increased apparently by unsatisfactory political conditions. The surplus human beings sought sustenance by emigration, and formed colonies over the coasts of the Mediterranean and the Black Sea. New markets were opened to trade to an extent undreamed of before. Numerous inventions were made in various departments of life. The arts of shipbuilding and navigation advanced step after step. Weights and measures of uniform and trustworthy standards were brought into use. Money was coined; and trade, freed from the trammels of barter, rose by leaps and bounds. Banks were started, with agencies and representatives in different countries.

One result of all this was a great increase of wealth in general; a steady flow of population from the country to the large towns; the establishment of important mercantile and shipping establishments and of extensive factories. Another result is to be found in the acute trade rivalries of the time and the recurrent commercial crises; in the bitter and bewildered complaints preserved to us in ancient literature about the number of respectable citizens who fall hopelessly into debt; in the rise, at various centres, of a town proletariat. It is much the same story in Solon; in the Hebrew prophets from Amos onwards; in the records of the class warfare of early Rome.

Concurrently with this economic development runs a political development. The main factors are the same in all the progressive towns. The commercial class and the manufacturing class—sometimes one, sometimes both, and both in varying degrees of strength—wrest the power from the old landed nobility. But in most places, and notably in Athens, they do so only at the price of constant concessions to the Demos—that is, to the artisan and day labourer, the common sailor and the unemployed proletariat.

To take the most typical instance. In Athens, commerce and manufacture join forces and gradually conquer the agrarian interest, though in the course of the struggle the peasant and the noble have made common cause. The law, which used to be the privileged possession and secret of the nobles, is first published so that all may know it, then liberalized in the interest of the commercial classes, who proceed next to wrest victoriously from the nobles both the franchise and the chief political power. But the price they pay for this success is that they have to carry the battle further. Both laws and franchise are by successive steps further democratized, till the predominant factor in political life is no longer the noble, no longer the rich merchant or manufacturer, but the mere free citizen. And what are these free citizens, as a matter of fact, at the time, say, of Pericles and Cleon? They are no longer well-to-do yeomen or prosperous mechanics. The great slum and dock population forms numerically the chief part of them, and the average member of the Athenian lower class, though politically free and in voting power actually supreme, is economically helpless, and apt, as the result of any serious disturbance in trade or agriculture, to be out of work and go to bed supperless. Government is to a great extent carried on or controlled by a chronically discontented working-class.

EXPLOITATION OF INFERIOR RACES

It is a curious and pathetic study how in the great flush of democratic triumph, when free Athens won independence for Greece, cleared the sea of pirates, and established throughout her empire the reign of freedom and equal law, the people seemed to think that by the mere breaking of the bonds that had crippled them everything was won. There was then no thought of commercial distress, or of what we now call the Social Question. One fact is very typical. The old Attic law especially forbids begging, that characteristic trade of mediæval societies, and enjoins that every man, being now free, must work and support himself. It took only some two generations to break through that illusion. The old Democrats saw with bewildered irritation new politicians come forward and claim that not only the infirm and afflicted, but the ordinary able-bodied citizen must in some form or other be kept from destitution by the State, and that without any stigma on his honour. It might be payment for attending the popular jury-courts or for serving on the political council; it might be large relief works like (probably) the Erechtheum, but in some form subsistence must be guaranteed to the ordinary citizen, and if the price of commodities rose, as it did in war-time, why then the public payment must be increased in proportion!

Throughout all this period slave labour has been steadily growing and actively accentuating all the

LIBERALISM AND THE EMPIRE

disorders of the time. Let us see the process by which this came about.

Commerce and manufacture on a large scale are still flourishing. Nicias employs a thousand miners; a small middle-class master like Demosthenes' father has thirty specially skilled swordsmiths in his little factory of arms. Taxes are light; trade is practically free; the demand for labour is very great. But what sort of labour will the employer prefer? Will he take the poor Athenian or Corinthian citizen, who is in law his full equal and in politics probably his opponent, and his successful opponent; who insists on such wages and such conditions as he considers fitting for a free citizen, and is prepared, if anything goes wrong with either, to prosecute his employer without hesitation; who is really not trained to factory life, and demands recreation and independence as a matter of course? Or will he turn to the East and the North, where long chains of successful Greek colonies have one after another reduced their neighbouring barbarians to subjection, have killed out the wilder and unworkable tribes, have tamed and trained and bred those that were submissive and useful? Our supposed employer will find there hundreds of operatives on the market, some of them already trained in various trades, most of them accustomed to complete obedience, all of them definitely his legal inferiors, with no right to prosecute him or complain of him or disobey him,

EXPLOITATION OF INFERIOR RACES

unless, indeed, he should treat them with quite exceptional cruelty; above all, all *his* to do what he likes with and exploit to the limits of their health and strength. The employers did not hesitate. They bought Scythians, Thracians, Phrygians, Lydians, and left the Athenian unemployed to enjoy their freedom and their leisure. The normal supply of slaves by way of trade with the East continually proved insufficient to meet the demand. It was reinforced by the subjugated aborigines of the Thracian and Scythian 'hinterlands.' Every war brought quantities more upon the market. And if all these sources failed, as they sometimes did, there was still the scum of the seafaring population of the Levant to go kidnapping and raiding in barbarous regions for the indispensable commodity.

In Rome the social development was on the whole very similar, and can be summed up in a few sentences. The main difference lay in the preliminary conditions. The most progressive Greek States were maritime, industrial, commercial. Rome was in the time of Regulus an agricultural community. The Rome which began the conquest of the Mediterranean world was a nation of peasants—yeomen, farmers, and free labourers; the Rome that emerged from that conquest had scarcely any free peasantry left. At first immense riches flowed into Italy, especially into the capital. The town population grew, and with it the demand for corn. A momentary stimulation of native agriculture was followed by the competition of more favoured countries. Sicily, Africa, and Egypt soon beat Italy out of the field; only a few districts, such as the valley of the Po and the Roman Campagna, were able to compete at all. Meantime, while agricultural life was getting more difficult, the peasants were being estranged from the soil. They were constantly engaged in military service, and tended to place their hopes of fortune in the spoils of war rather than the fruits of husbandry. Above all, when they came back from long campaigns abroad the veterans had forgotten their farming. Doubtless other causes were at work also. It is at any rate certain that the Italian husbandmen fell into a normal and recurrent condition of distress, and sold or lost their land in ever-increasing numbers. Some of the land became derelict, some was bought up cheap or seized as bankrupt stock by speculators and capitalists, and worked by enormous gangs of those foreign slaves whom the centuries of war were making a drug in the market. In the last period of the Republic, when the new economic conditions had definitely established themselves, Italy found herself still an agricultural and pastoral country; but the owners of land were very few, and the shepherds, labourers, and overseers were foreign slaves. The 'Plantation System,' as it has been called, was imported from Carthage. Doubtless in the hands of a

EXPLOITATION OF INFERIOR RACES

masterful and unsympathetic people like the Romans it led to enormous cruelties. Economically, though apparently cheap to start with, and the cause of many individuals making great fortunes, it ultimately reduced a large part of Italy to a waste of beggars and brigands, and perished from its own wastefulness. But it had the merit of being well organized. There is surely some significance in the well-attested fact that in the regular daily rations of the plantation slaves the ordinary labourer received a higher allowance than the bailiff or overseer. For such beasts of burden must be scientifically fed, and the labourer doing the most wasting bodily work has to be equipped for it with the greatest amount of victuals!

One may ask, before passing to the modern side of our subject, what kinds of criticism were actually raised, or what protests made, in antiquity against the institution of slave labour. The slaves, poor creatures! protested as well as they could. In the early days of the system there were insurrections on a large scale—blind paroxysms of desperation, for the most part, which were crushed with all the appalling severity of which Roman pride and capitalist fear were capable. But soon, from whatever cause, the insurrections ceased. Individual slaves could still murder their master if chance offered, could sometimes run away, could at least hang themselves; but united action had become impossible, and, like most extreme suffering, their misery was inarticulate.

Did the free workmen and peasants protest? Doubtless they did, but we hear on the whole little about it. In some few States of Greece, such as Locris, the free workmen were strong enough to keep out slave labour altogether; but it is a noteworthy comment on frail human nature that on the whole the highly intelligent Greek artisans and peasants could not act with any self-sacrifice or public spirit upon this vital question. The ordinary man, it would seem, tolerated a system that was disastrous to his class, because he was tempted by the prospect of possibly rising above his class. He might some day get a slave of his own, and then live in ease like his betters.

The protest of the dispossessed Italian peasant is accidentally preserved to us in the celebrated words quoted by Plutarch from Tiberius Gracchus: "The wild beasts of Italy have their lairs and hiding-places, but the men who fight and die for Italy wander houseless and homeless with their wives and children, and have nothing of their own except the air and the sunlight. When the Generals before a battle bid them fight for the tombs and shrines of their ancestors, the Generals are talking lies. They have no ancestral shrines, no ancestral graves any more; they only fight to defend the wealth and the luxury of strangers. The 'masters of the world' themselves have not a clod of earth to call their own."

Affecting and grand words; but there is practically no suggestion of a remedy, no condemnation at all of slavery in itself.

If we turn from practical to speculative protests, many, perhaps most, Greek philosophers from the fifth century B.C. onwards condemned the institution of slavery in itself as 'contrary to nature.' Some of the democratic sophists, like Alcidamas, proposed its actual abolition. But for us it is more instructive to consider the arguments on the other side, the defences of slavery.

The best is perhaps that given by Aristotle. The offspring of an absolute monarchy, educated in the school of the mordant and anti-democratic Plato, he is peculiarly strong and lucid when criticising democratic sentimentalists. 'Slavery,' so we may condense his various statements, 'is emphatically according to nature. Put down a dozen Greeks in a small village of barbarians, and you will soon find the Greeks instinctively giving orders and the barbarians instinctively carrying them out—that is, one race is born to rule, other races to obey.' The slavery of Greek to Greek he of course condemns, just as he condemns cruelty.

It is certainly difficult to deny Aristotle's premises. It is a thing abundantly proved by experience that on the whole white men are 'superior' to black, brown, red, and yellow men—that is to say, that on the whole the first-mentioned colour tends to rule and the other colours to obey. But obviously, a modern theorist will object, the premises are not enough to support the conclusion; an inferior and a servant need not be a slave. The answer, of course, is that Aristotle was not afraid of the word 'slave,' and used it far more lightly and freely than we care to do. His own admirable definition of the term as 'a live tool' seems to cover exactly the same ground as our word 'exploit.' In so far as a person is 'exploited'—that is, in so far as he is used for another's interest without any regard for his own— he is, according to Aristotle, a slave. The ancients would certainly have regarded not only the enforced labour of the Matabele, but the ordinary indentured labour of 'niggers' in Kimberley, Kanakas in Queensland, and coolies in India, Demerara, Fiji, and the like, as slave labour.

Turning now to modern times, it is worth while asking what symptoms there are, if any, of a tendency to use inferior alien labour in at all the same spirit and for the same purposes as the ancients used their hosts of imported slaves.

The most obviously or apparently analogous cases will be those of definite legal slavery, acknowledged still in some German colonies, in the Congo State, and in the Zanzibar protectorate. The forced labour of the Matabele was very similar—that is, the servants were obtained by force as well as detained by force—except that, being less regular and legal, it was probably accompanied by greater violence and more systematic fraud.

The 'corvée' or forced labour system, which implied a kind of formal, though very limited, slavery, is said to be still practised in some parts of British India, and exists in a very severe form in Natal. In Egypt it was abolished by us some years ago, but seems—though the statement has been denied—to have been reintroduced during the Soudan campaign under irregular and therefore exasperating conditions (*Daily News*, March 8, 1899). In the Soudan itself we have, of course, recently proclaimed the formal abolition of slavery. The system we propose to substitute for it has been lucidly described by Sir Rudolph Slatin in an interview which appeared in several newspapers.[1] 'The nigger is a lazy beast,' said Slatin, 'and must be compelled to work—compelled by Government.' 'How?' asked his interlocutor. 'With a stick,' was Slatin's reply. Those who have followed the course of Slatin's singular career can perhaps form some notion of the probable weight of that stick!

But the cases of formal slavery are, after all, exceptional conditions, small in extent, and pretty generally condemned by public opinion. For our

---

[1] For instance, *Daily Mail*, March 11, 1899.

present purpose they may be almost neglected. There are two really extensive and organic systems of exploiting the labour of inferior races.

The first is simply the old Græco-Roman system improved and modified—the system of importing destitute or semi-destitute aliens to countries where they can serve us. The difference is that the ancients used undisguised force throughout the whole process; we use economic pressure to get our labourers, though we mostly use force to keep them. The simplest case is the system of indenture as applied to Indian and Chinese coolies, and to Polynesians or Kanakas. The labourer voluntarily signs an agreement for a term of years, and is shipped off to a foreign country, where he is, for most purposes, not under the ordinary law, but under special indenture regulations. His freedom is curtailed in every direction; but, on the other hand, his wages are secured and his general condition inspected by Government. He is looked after when he is sick, protected against extremes of cruelty and dishonesty on the part of his master, and taken home again at the end of his time. The system works well in places like Fiji, where the area is small, supervision easy, and the Government not dependent upon the employers. It works ill in large continental regions, such as Queensland, where these conditions are reversed. About 15,000 indentured coolies leave India every year. About 10,000 Kanakas go from

EXPLOITATION OF INFERIOR RACES

Polynesia to Queensland every year. For the Chinese coolies it is difficult to find figures.

The Chinese represent, for the most part, another class of subject-workers not actually indentured, but living by labour in foreign countries, and forming a despised alien community. As domestic servants, as market-gardeners, as shopkeepers, as miners, the evidence seems to show that they form a praiseworthy and valuable element in any society; but the democracies of America and of Australia, resenting the excellences of the Chinese even more than their defects, have passed prohibitive laws against their immigration. The American laws have reduced the number of resident Chinese to 107,000; the Australian, reinforced by irregular brutalities from the British inhabitants, have brought them down to very low figures indeed—Victoria, 9,000; New Zealand, 3,000; New South Wales, 1,500; and so on. In the northern territory, however, where the poll-tax is only £30 a head, there are 12,000 Chinese amid a very small white population, and in the Straits Settlements, where there is no prohibition, they swarm in at the rate of 200,000 a year! Of course, they also return home in great numbers.

Within very narrow limits alien labour other than Chinese is imported by leading European countries. Swarms of Poles come into Germany for the harvest, swarms of Irish into England. In industrial crises the plan is often mooted of bringing in cheap aliens by the thousand and doing without the stiff-necked British workman. An attempt was made about 1890 to man some works at Troon entirely with Poles, and there are complaints now (May, 1900) in South Lanarkshire about the increasing employment of Poles in the mines. Some shiploads of negro servants are said to be at this moment arriving in London from the United States. But these plans have apparently never yet been successfully carried out. In America, indeed, there are threatenings of serious trouble in connection with the employment of negroes to do 'white men's work.' The Governor of Illinois in 1898 actually expelled a multitude of blacks who had been imported by a mining trust, and threatened publicly that if another such mob were introduced: 'I care not on what railroad it comes, or for whom; I will meet it at the State line, and shoot it to pieces with Gatling guns.' The annual invasion of foreign Jews into East London and other British towns is a matter of small moment at present. Foreign sailors, on the other hand, form a very numerous class in the British mercantile marine. The figures are (1896) 33,000 odd foreigners —to whom must be added a large number of Lascars and similar 'British subjects'—out of a total of 242,000 persons employed on British ships.

Two particularly instructive cases of the employment of aliens are to be found in the *Bulletin of the U.S. Labour Bureau*. The first of these is that of

EXPLOITATION OF INFERIOR RACES

domestic service in America, an employment which is increasingly felt to be beneath the dignity of the free white American. Unfortunately, the *Bulletin* does not state what actual numbers of native white Americans are engaged in domestic service, but from the fact that year after year 60 per cent. of the female immigrants go straight into domestic service, together with the notoriously large employment of negroes, one can conclude that as a normal thing the intelligent, highly-paid American is actually in the position of a ruling race, and is served and attended by negroes and alien immigrants very much as the ancient Athenian was served by a Thracian or an Asiatic. The second case is connected with the conditions of Italian immigration (*Bulletin* for March, 1897). An Act passed in 1864 gave employers the right to import foreign labour under contract. The American contractor used to procure the requisite gangs of Italian peasants by means of an Italian immigration agent, called a 'banker,' who obtained a commission on their passage money, besides making a profit by entertaining them when they arrived in America. In the next stage the 'banker' becomes himself a contractor, and exploits Italian immigrants on his own account; he is then called a 'padrone.' The 'padrone' received the workmen when they came, boarded them, kept their wages for them, professed to maintain them when out of work, involved them inextricably in debt, and established a condition of 'semi-slavery for the workman.' This 'padrone' system has been forbidden by law and otherwise disturbed, with the result that the 'padrone' has now brought himself into harmony with American institutions by calling himself a 'boss,' while the commission he receives is described by the new Italian word *bossatura*.

In all the above cases the alien labourer is imported. But—and this forms the second of what we have called the really extensive and organic systems of exploiting inferior races—the great field for the working of the alien in modern times is the alien's own country. In this one fact lies, perhaps, the greatest and most fortunate difference between the ancient and the modern conditions. Let us dwell upon it for a moment. In ancient times the employer would not, if he could help it, go away from his own country to employ Libyans or Scythians in their native places. If he left home, it was not so easy to come back. He was practically in exile. In the second place, he was not sufficiently master of his slaves in their own country. If they were all of one nation and all at home, they might rebel or break loose. If a strong Government prevented that, it was at any rate much easier for individual slaves to escape—a consideration always of the utmost importance. It is mentioned, for instance, by Mungo Park, that among the natives of North-West Africa the price of a slave rises steadily in proportion to the distance that divides him from his own country.

EXPLOITATION OF INFERIOR RACES

In modern times, the increasing ease of communication has enabled white men to go abroad to all parts of the earth without suffering much real exile, and without losing the prospect of returning home at will. Our Governments, judged by ancient standards, are miraculously strong; our superior weapons make rebellions almost impossible. Consequently, we do not attempt to import blacks, coolies, and Polynesians into Great Britain. The opposition of the working-classes at home would be furious; and even if that obstacle were overcome, the coloured men would die too fast in our climate. The whole economic conditions are in favour of working the coloured man in his own home. It may also be permitted to us to reflect that, when the slave or subject is among his own people, there must remain to him a large remnant of life which is not utterly poisoned by the advent of the white master.

The whole of tropical mining, and almost the whole of tropical agriculture—the raising of rice, coffee, sugar, and the like—are carried out by gangs of cheap labourers of inferior race under the rule of white men. And not only in India, where it is a natural outcome of the system of Government, but in most of the semi-civilized nations of the world, white men can be found directing the ill-paid and often forced labour of the inhabitants.

As to South Africa, I should for many reasons prefer to be silent. That region is so wrapped in

LIBERALISM AND THE EMPIRE

concealment and misrepresentation at the present moment, that it is hard to find any certain groundwork to build upon. Still, the South African systems are altogether too important to be omitted, and their main lines seem to be tolerably clear. The capital feature of South African life, as every traveller observes, is that all unskilled work is done by black people. That is the rudimentary and essential condition of slavery, and is doubtless quite unavoidable. As to direct cruelty, the laws are, as usual, a great deal more humane than the facts, though some of the laws themselves sound a little odd to English ears. A white master in Cape Colony is not allowed to flog his own servants, a Bill which gave him that power having recently been defeated; but he can send them to a magistrate to be imprisoned for negligence, insolence, or misbehaviour. A coloured man in Natal cannot walk on the footpath or go in a tramcar, and so on.

Yet a radical improvement in the laws would probably do more harm than good. The essential cause of cruelty and oppression is not the law, but, to quote Mr. Bryce's careful and temperate description, 'the strong feeling of dislike and contempt—one might almost say of hostility—which the bulk of the whites show to their black neighbours.' This curious feeling, a compound in which physical repulsion, race-hatred, and pride of birth seem to be accentuated by actual shame and remorse, appears to be even

EXPLOITATION OF INFERIOR RACES

stronger in South Africa than in most similar societies. Yet, on the whole, the cruelties to blacks in those regions seem to be less atrocious than in Australia. The following case, which I select from half a dozen as having been already published by Mr. Bryce, reminds one of Queensland: 'A shocking case of the kind occurred a few years ago in the Eastern Province. A white farmer—an Englishman, not a Boer—flogged his Kaffir servant so severely that the latter died; and when the culprit was put on his trial and acquitted by a white jury, his white neighbours escorted him home with a band of music.'

Two African systems of exploiting black labour seem to promise great developments—the compound and the location. At Kimberley the natives are herded, some 3,000 together, in compounds or huge enclosures, covered with wire netting, and having no egress except an underground passage to the mines. These special precautions are taken in order to prevent the blacks from stealing diamonds. They buy their food on the truck system from the company, and cannot go outside for any purpose. They are imprisoned in this way till the end of their contract time, which may in some cases be as short as three months.

The location system, which is contemplated at Johannesburg, consists in inducing large numbers of natives to settle with their families in the neighbourhood where their work is required. Once there, they are prevented by law from having enough land to live upon, prevented from leaving the locality by a rigorous system of passes, deliberately reduced to destitution by a Hut Tax and a Labour Tax, and thus forced into the mines to work at twopence a day, or whatever wage the Chamber of Mines thinks fit. As Lord Grey puts it: 'Means must be sought to induce the natives to seek spontaneously (*sic!*) employment at the mines, and to work willingly for long periods of more or less continuous service.' The means he proposes are those mentioned above—a Hut Tax in money, which the native will be unable to pay except by resorting to the mines, and a Labour Tax on all able-bodied natives who are unable to show a certificate for four months' work in the year. This is also the principle of the Glen Grey Act, passed in Cape Colony in 1894. The penalty for non-payment of the tax is imprisonment with hard labour—that is, we reduce the native to destitution by special laws in order to force him to work for us, and if he will not work then we can kidnap him!

This system is so ingenious and elastic, offers such opportunities for the fraud which is normal in contracts between whites and blacks, and does its work of gradual demoralization so insidiously, and with so little shock to public feeling, that we may expect it to spread and flourish in other continents, almost in

EXPLOITATION OF INFERIOR RACES

the manner of the Roman plantation system. Like that system, the compound wishes to care for the welfare of its beasts. The employers—some of them, no doubt, made rich by selling liquor to blacks elsewhere—have set their faces against the supply of alcohol to their own workers. But, like the Romans, they will probably be disappointed. As a matter of fact, the mines have hitherto been the great centres of drinking, as well as of even more degrading corruption. Mr. Scully, for instance (Blue Book G. 31, 1899, p. 76), notes the 'deplorable demoralization' of natives returning from the mines, 'brutish in their knowledge,' and the increase, or introduction, among those to whom they return of phthisis, rheumatism, pulmonary diseases, and syphilis.

In military operations, again, we of the British Empire depend to a quite enormous extent upon soldiers of alien race, more, possibly, than any State since Carthage. Nearly all our African fighting before the present war, and most of our Indian fighting, has been done for us by natives. The great victories of Clive over the French, which we are accustomed to regard as proofs of British strength or valour, were almost entirely victories of Sepoys over Sepoys. The economic situation is really the same as in the other cases. We cannot spare more of the ruling race to fight. We take instead some naturally warlike savages, train them, officer them, and make them do the fighting for us. They like it, they are cheap, and we do not mind so much when they are killed. In fact, it is a plan excellent in all respects save two. In the first place, if ever a time of need should come, and we should cease to be obviously the winning side, such armies might tend to fight against us rather than for us; and, in the second place, the continual employment of these uniformed savages probably tends to lead British warfare in various unmentionable details rather too close to that of savages without uniform.[1]

[1] To take two cases that have come before me on two successive days while revising this essay. (1) An advertisement: 'Blank's Revolvers; the only pistols approved and adopted by the British Government for service requirements. . . . Blank's patent man-stopping revolver bullets, adopted by Her Majesty's Government. . . . *The expansive principle has been carried to its greatest extent.* . . . Upon entering the flesh the front of the bullet acts like a wadding-punch, cutting out a clean round hole which does not close up. Expansion commences immediately, and after a bullet has travelled six inches it produces a jagged hole from 3 in. to 4 in. in diameter. . . . Proved their efficiency at Elandslaagte' (*Westminster Gazette,* May 19, 1900). (2) A speech of Captain Lauder, Seaforth Highlanders, sympathetically reported in the *Daily News* of May 17, 1900 : 'We swore to be revenged. And so well did we avenge them that Lord Roberts himself wondered why the 72nd never took any prisoners. He said to our General, Sir James Baker, "How in the world, sir, is it that all the other regiments in the division take so many prisoners, and the 72nd never take any ?" Sir James Baker knew the reason, but he simply said, "No, the 72nd never take any prisoners." The Captain, with the story-teller's

EXPLOITATION OF INFERIOR RACES

It may be objected to these remarks that they only contain an account, and that a very sketchy and imperfect account, of certain forms of alien labour; that the systems described, whether good or bad, are not systems of legal slavery. But my whole argument is that the legal status of slavery has little to do with the question; the essential object of both the ancient slave-system and these divers modern makeshifts is a world-wide division of labour among breeds of men, the inferior work going to the inferior races, the higher work to the higher and more highly-paid races. The ancient employer did not specially want legal slaves; he wanted cheap alien labour, and that could only be had in the form of slaves. The modern employer can, as a rule, get his cheap alien labour by processes less wasteful, less shocking to outside opinion, and less disastrously cruel. But the essence of the demand is the same, and the essence of the thing supplied is the same.

A man does not become a slave, if you come to think of the essence of the matter, through a legal process. He becomes a slave when he is brought into contact with a superior race, which can and will use him as a tool. Three principal tests occur to one by which to recognise slavery; they are the three points which more than others are noted by

---

art, left his hearers to infer the rest.' This implies a savage rather than a European standard.

ancient authors about the actual slaves of antiquity:

First, whatever work the slave does is despised; free men refuse to do it. We have noticed some instances of this already. It may be added that in Sydney in the seventies, before the exclusion of the Chinese, white people objected to washing clothes or keeping market-gardens, on the definite ground that those employments were Chinamen's work.

Secondly, enslaved people lapse into a state of extreme degradation and immorality. That is often remarked in antiquity, and is observed by modern travellers. For instance, Father Ohrwalder notices that the various races from which the slaves of the Dervishes were drawn were in their independent state entirely free from the destructive immorality which characterized them in slavery. The Indian coolies in Fiji, the compound blacks in Kimberley, the Chinese in Sydney and San Francisco, are notorious for extreme corruption and degradation. So are the natives of Australia who have been much in contact with the whites, so are the West Africans, so are in general, I suspect, all inferior races throughout the world as soon as ever they are faced with the paralyzing presence of the white man. Dirt in his eyes, they soon become as dirt in their own.

Thirdly, and this is a point very similar to the last, enslaved people very largely tend to despair and die. One remembers the complaints in Roman writers of the ridiculously frivolous pretexts on which slaves would commit suicide. A slave accidentally lost a napkin. 'Why, if I had found it out,' says his master, 'I would only have given him half a dozen cuts with a whip, and the fool must needs hang himself!' You see what it means? That life is so low, and poor, and vile, and hopeless, that a feather in the scale makes the slave throw it away. You will hear exactly similar stories from Englishmen about negroes in Africa and about Hindoos, and I have heard at first hand some startling cases in the South Seas. This is the state of mind which makes races die out. If we hear of a race like the Tasmanians or the Red Indians disappearing quietly, under no stress of persecution, no massacres or poisonings, we are perhaps inclined to look upon the process as a harmless and painless one. It is not so. Those men and women who look broken-down by the time they are thirty, who leave no children behind them, who have forgotten their fishing and their hunting and their old rude forms of art, who sit (as I have seen one or two) with heads bowed, doing nothing, saying nothing, in a world in which there is no longer anything they can call their own —those men and women are, I think, engaged in a process that we sometimes read about but do not often see: they are dying of despair.

No; if we come to analyze the meaning of slavery, it is in something of that sort that it will be found.

LIBERALISM AND THE EMPIRE

It is, as Aristotle said, a fact in nature, a fact which can be altered and mitigated in various ways, but which consists ultimately in the juxtaposition of a 'superior' and an 'inferior' breed of men. It is important to notice in passing that these words 'superior' and 'inferior' have in this context little, if any, purely moral connotation. One race is 'up,' and the other is 'down'; and the 'ups' not only often use their position like fiends, but usually tend to suffer a good deal of moral deterioration from the mere fact of that position.

In the fields of prophecy it is not wise to venture far. It looks as if the use of aliens for unskilled labour was certain to increase. The rapid rise of cotton-factories in India—the numbers in the Bombay Presidency have trebled in ten years—suggests that they may also be found suitable for some kinds of skilled labour. On the other hand, we may be fairly sure that the English democracy will never allow coloured labourers to be imported in any large numbers into this country; and that the Australian and American democracies, whether or no they are sinning against the light of political economy in excluding the Chinese, will never within the measurable future repent of their sin. For the rest, one may be confident that the American and Australian dread of alien competition has exaggerated the danger. The effect of the freer exploitation of coloured labour will be, as it has hitherto been,

EXPLOITATION OF INFERIOR RACES

analogous to the effect of Free Trade and of machinery. There will be particular and temporary conditions of distress; but, on the whole, many necessaries and conveniences of life will be cheapened, and the standard of comfort raised for the white working-man.

There is one further question which would once have been asked, and which may still occur to a few old-fashioned idealists. Is this subjection of the inferior races to be absolute and eternal, or is there any prospect of our educating them up to the point of freedom and self-government? The question is a distasteful one to the modern politician. We used once to vaunt our intention of achieving this end in India; we are bound by solemn and reiterated engagements to strive after it in Egypt. It is, or was, held as a kind of ideal, a shadowy part of our 'Imperial Mission' elsewhere. Meantime, no political party with any prospect of holding office seems to have the faintest hope of achieving that end, or even much desire of working towards it. A similar problem occurred in the Roman Empire, and Gibbon reflects (end of chapter xxxi., on Gaul) that if the provinces had ever really been vitalized and trained to self-government, instead of being administered by despotic bureaucracies, that Empire might never have fallen. We are at present shirking the herculean task, just as Rome shirked it. It seems to demand qualities which are not cultivated by such nations as Rome or England.

LIBERALISM AND THE EMPIRE

In the meantime, let us recall for a moment our main subject, and the meaning of the words '*servus*' and 'slave.' A slave is ultimately a man spared in war; a man whom you might kill, but whom you prefer to keep, in order to make him work for you. It is abundantly clear, if one considers the question, that this has historically been the position of most of the subject races in the British Empire. And it is in a sense their condition still. Those whom we cannot utilize we exterminate; those whom we can utilize we protect, and often enable to increase in numbers. Tasmanians were useless, and are all dead. The Bhils are mostly dead. Australians were all but useless, good only for horse-taming and man-tracking, and they are dwindling to nothing. Red Indians, in spite of enormous care, and the large sums of money that a penitent Government now spends upon them, are dying gradually. In Africa, those blacks for whom we have some use tend, with certain exceptions, to increase and multiply; those for whom we have no use die by drink, by war, by economic pressure, and by the mere discouragement which works like poison in the veins of a race that finds its occupation gone.

The cruelties perpetrated by white men upon coloured men are, almost wherever and however they meet, stupendous. But the coloured men who are worked under definite rules and indentures are far better off than those who cannot be worked at all, or those who, under conditions of nominal equality,

EXPLOITATION OF INFERIOR RACES

are forced to work, unprotected, beneath the hand of any chance master. The Kanakas in Queensland, under the old indenture system, were no doubt treated both harshly and unfairly. They were kidnapped, they were brutally used, they were cheated of their miserable earnings. And it may be doubted whether the improvement of their condition under the present system is as great as is alleged. Yet they were probably better off than the Matabele forced labourers, strong men held down under a weak and irregular system, which had necessarily to be backed up by fraud or violence. But go, if you dare, into a searching comparison between the treatment of the Queensland Kanakas, who were useful beasts of burden, and that of the Queensland aborigines, who were regarded as vermin, and you will bless the lot of the half-enslaved Kanaka.

Let no one delude himself with the fancy that, though the German Dr. Peters may flog his concubines to death, though Frenchmen in the New Hebrides may twist the flesh off their servants' backs with pincers, though our own newspapers may revel in reported horrors from the old Transvaal or the Congo Free State, Englishmen, Scotchmen, and Irishmen are quite of another breed. Not to speak of strange and unpleasant dealings with black women, I myself knew well one man who told me he had shot blacks at sight. I have met a man who boasted of having spilt poisoned meal along a road near a black-

LIBERALISM AND THE EMPIRE

fellows' camp, in order to get rid of them like rats. My brother was the guest of a man in Queensland who showed him a particular bend of a river where he had once, as a jest, driven a black family, man, woman, and children, into the water among a shoal of crocodiles. My father has described to me his fruitless efforts to get men punished in New South Wales in old days for offering hospitality to blacks and giving them poisoned meat. I received, while first writing these notes, a newspaper from Perth, giving an account of the trial of some Coolgardie miners for beating to death with heavy bits of wood a black woman and boy who had been unable to show them the way. The bodies were found with the shoulder-blades in shivers, and the judge observed that such cases were getting too common! These atrocities are not necessarily the work of isolated and extraordinary villains. Two of the men mentioned above were rather good men than bad. Nor have I mentioned the worst class of outrages. It is only the old trail of the superior race, the eternal dripping of the blood of the weaker, which had recorded the expansion of Aryan and Semite in the old world before it passed to mark the white man's steps in America, North and South, in the South Sea Islands, in Africa.

What way is there of meeting a situation such as this? Perhaps there is none. At least, the best solution seems to me to demand certain national qualities which neither England nor, as far as I know, any European nation either possesses or seeks to acquire. But at least we must face the facts frankly, and apply lenitives. The coloured races whose lands we invade cannot remain free men. The white man who lives among them, do what we will to control him from Westminster—and those who wish to control him are a small and perhaps a diminishing party—will either force the coloured men to serve him, or else sweep them from his path. Let us help him, in order that we may control him. Let us not jib at special native legislation; let us increase the sphere of our protecting codes. Only let us insist on having the codes administered, as far as possible, by Imperial officers, who, though often ignorant and unsympathetic, will be free from the disastrous bias of the colonists themselves.[1]

[1] The very able appeal made by the Aborigines Protection Society to the Colonial Secretary on May 11, 1900, begins with recommending : 'A declaration that all natives . . . within Her Majesty's dominions in South Africa are in the position of wards of the Crown, and that any Royal Proclamations and Acts of the Imperial Parliament affecting them shall not be liable to alteration by any local Legislature without the deliberate sanction of the Crown and Imperial Parliament, in effective compliance with the right of veto at present reserved but rarely exercised.' The rest of the document is mainly concerned with arrangements for native reserves, on the Basutoland model, with the removal of a number of specific abuses, and with provisions for bridging

LIBERALISM AND THE EMPIRE

Let us frankly abandon for the present the ideal of one universal British law—we have never really acted upon it. Let us recognise the dependent condition of the natives, help towards liberty those that can be helped, and defend the rest by every possible means from masters who are sure, at the best, to exploit them harshly. There is in the world a hierarchy of races. The bounds of it are not, of course, absolute and rigid, as the negro judges in America and the many eminent natives of India show; but, on the whole, it seems that those nations which eat more, claim more, and get higher wages, will direct and rule the others, and the lower work of the world will tend in the long-run to be done by the lower breeds of men. Thus much we of the ruling colour will no doubt accept as obvious. It is probable, too, in spite of the present reaction in favour of harshness, that in course of time, partly by better organization, partly by increased publicity and the action of European opinion upon the colonists, partly by the mere extirpation of the most ill-used races, the presence of the white man will tend to entail less extreme suffering upon his subjects. The great question is whether we are able, either by a gigantic improvement in the British national character, or by constant and lively super-

---

over the dangerous interval between 'complete tribal institutions' and 'civilization.'

EXPLOITATION OF INFERIOR RACES

vision, or by some ingenious scheme for combining the interests of ruler and subject, to induce our colonists and our home public to labour honourably and intelligently for the welfare of those weak human beings to whom we fulfil almost the rôle of Providence, or whether we prefer to treat them chiefly as means of satisfying our desire for riches, our love of glory, or our instinct for authority and command. No doubt that extravagant self-conceit which every nation thinks fit to encourage in itself and to rebuke in others has long ago answered this question in our favour. But the answer is premature. The task is barely begun, and not begun so very brilliantly. If ever in the lifetime of the world a duty has been laid upon a nation, a great and manifest obligation lies on us towards our subject-peoples, the duty of endeavouring by strenuous and honest sympathy, justice, and even magnanimity, to obliterate our cruel conquests, and justify our world-wide usurpation. On the way in which we respond to that call of duty, more than on any other single criterion, depends the verdict that history must pass upon us, whether to proclaim us the greatest and most beneficent of nations, or merely to dismiss us as one more group in the long dark flight of transient and unprofitable conquerors, 'birds of prey and of passage,' at whose final disappearance Humanity will raise her bent head and utter a sigh of relief.

COLONIAL AND FOREIGN POLICY

IN the hour of exhaustion and defeat, Liberalism has never entirely lost the fortitude which it owes to the trials of its novitiate. The faith of what has been in the first stages of nearly every great foreign trouble a minority in public opinion, exposed to the vehemence of popular antagonism, almost vindictively pursued with the passion which inflames the exaggeration of a virtue, it has been held with a courage and a tenacity of which the secret is to be found in the bitter struggles of its earliest champions. Its vitality is explained by the compensations of Nature. If it has passed long years of discipline in the rough school of adversity, it had already proved itself brave, steadfast, and persistent in its first strenuous energies. For not even our political sky is blacker than that under which Fox withstood the policy which devoted the strength of England to the appetites and the rancours of Europe, and diverted the splendid promise of the Revolution into the catastrophe of the Empire. No single circumstance of hardship or discouragement was wanting. The normal ties of politics had been broken. Fox had suffered the public dissolution of a friendship more than a quarter of a century old, consecrated by the peculiar memories of common action in great crises of State. There were left to him, it is true, the brilliant talents of an Erskine, a Sheridan, and a Grey. But Portland, Fitzwilliam, and Windham had followed Burke, and to add to his own small party a single vote was a miracle beyond the power of Fox himself. He had surrendered to principle a popularity to retain which he had sacrificed everything else. He watched the dismal fulfilment of all his dark predictions, as the long-protracted war became each day more disastrous to liberty in Europe and at home. And in those days of hot controversy, as in others, there were not lacking men whose blunt imaginations interpreted all temperaments by their own, and who divined little of the pain which they inflicted as they cut a sensitive nature to the quick with a cruel and senseless charge of treason, counting such accusations amongst the commonplace polemics of party warfare.

Those Englishmen who have inherited the Liberalism of Fox cannot reasonably complain if they share something of his hard lot. Their party is divided and doubtful; their popularity has waned, with little immediate prospect of a rally; their hopes of domestic reform are crumbling away before new imperious and distracting demands. Intolerance grows

LIBERALISM AND THE EMPIRE

apace—*mobilitate viget, virisque acquirit eundo*—and mob passions (rarely more ungovernable in the fiercest convulsions of southern cities) brawl, riot, and swagger in our midst, their turbulent revels countenanced by half our newspapers, and by some of our statesmen only perfunctorily blamed. Nor has a majority which professes to stand for a unanimous nation felt itself strong enough to refrain from raising the cry of 'Traitor!'

Pursue the analogy a little further, it will be said, and you will learn the fate of Liberalism. If Liberals choose the part of Fox, they cannot escape his eclipse. Mark the splendid waste of his genius—twenty years of his life exhausted in a fruitless struggle with the nightmares of a nation; his death surrounded by the abundant and unmistakable signs of the calamities he had seen written on the wall. Let Liberals measure their strength against the triumphant forces of Imperialism, and they can look for no better issue than a glorious defeat and the ineffectual stoicism of despair. And this is not the reasoning of our opponents only. Already within the party there are voices demanding new flags and new uniforms. The nation, we are warned, will not listen to men who will refuse it the pageants, the excitements, the spoils of foreign conquest. These things are the price of party victory. But our prophets reckon without the tradition and the changes of a century. Liberals do not appeal to-day to a tribunal of place-hunters competing for the favour of an obstinate Sovereign. Political democracy, with all its disappointments, remains at the worst something more than a multiplication of chances.[1] What oligarchy gains over democracy in administrative aptitude democracy recovers in the capacity for grasping and acting on simple moral principles. This is true even of that half-formed democracy under which we live—a democracy whose development is obstructed by the same material influences as arrest the free play of moral ideas. To despair is to forget all the lessons of the victorious courage of the Midlothian Campaign, a final and convincing demonstration of the enduring vitality of a Liberalism which has so often belied the premature epitaphs of politics.

A main cause of the precipitate abandonment of their traditions by many Liberals is to be found in a fatalism, a doctrine contemned by strenuous men and strenuous times, which has lately been erected with solemn honours into a political principle. It is not only amongst Conservatives that the new divinity claims its votaries. The pseudo-scientific jargon of 'manifest destiny,' 'inevitable development,' and the like—the vocabulary of men who see finality in each fugitive phase and phenomenon of public affairs—has invaded almost every school of

[1] Though even in this there is an element of hope, which Victor Hugo expressed in the soliloquy of Don Carlos in 'Hernani': 'Tout marche, et le hasard corrige le hasard.'

LIBERALISM AND THE EMPIRE

political thought; the politician casts his horoscope to find his principles; the ephemeral chatter of the street is hailed as the deliberate manifestation of the common will. Every volatile enthusiasm is mistaken for a great tidal wave destined to drown unpopular causes, and to toss statesmen aside like seaweed on the beach of our national life.

This habit of prophecy does much more than make our political astrologers look foolish; that it does effectually enough in time. The assumptions of Imperialist determinism have no greater claim to scientific accuracy than any of the predictions hazarded with no less assurance in the past which history has turned to ridicule. If our modern fatalist had been born a century earlier, and had applied to contemporary conditions the canons by which he now tests political contingencies, he would have arrived at any result rather than the truth. So acute an observer as Napoleon blundered; the chief Powers in 1815 rebuilt Europe on a foundation of sand; and we are not the more inclined to trust the judgment of our prophets of to-day, when we remember that it was a misunderstanding of the forces of nationality—the very forces these prophets discount as weak and declining—that ultimately brought to the ground the great edifice so elaborately constructed at Vienna. But the futility of this practice is of small consequence in comparison with its vicious results. If war is imminent, we are warned that no human power can stop it. When war breaks out, Providence and the enemy must divide the blame. If a conflict is inevitable, diplomacy becomes a mere incident, or, rather, well-timed irritation becomes a diplomatic art; and it is the business of a statesman, recognising that he cannot avoid a struggle, to arrange to provoke it at the moment most convenient to his own country —a desperate surrender to circumstances which more than a century ago Voltaire denounced as immoral. Thus, fatalism becomes a narcotic administered to the public conscience by the advocates of aggrandisement. Familiar with the mental and moral fatigue which prosperity induces in a nation, they present to an electorate hypnotized by material success the best of reasons for refusing to examine, to investigate, to thrash matters out. The doctrine provides a sonorous alias to all that is servile in our society. The creeping things in politics hail this high-sounding pretext for an inglorious acquiescence, and welcome so stately a disguise. What could be more consoling than to learn that an unpopular and difficult course leads to a blind alley?

But the whole temper of fatalism is foreign to the Liberal spirit. If Liberals are content with a moral somnolence, it is no wonder they have little taste for a creed which insists on nothing so strongly as the duty of developing just the active sense of responsibility that fatalism saps. Ulysses' bow was useless to men who were unable to draw it. The faith of Mr. Gladstone

LIBERALISM AND THE EMPIRE

sits ill upon a listless indifference to its great and vivifying principles. All the native fire and inspiration is gone out of his creed when it is invoked by Liberals who understand by Liberalism a disorderly collection of miscellaneous enthusiasms rather than an established attitude to the fundamental moralities of politics. For all idealism belongs to robust and virile natures; and the temper which governed the foreign policy associated with the name of Liberal during the nineteenth century was, above and before all things, idealist. They were Liberal statesmen who, in the name of the rights of nationality, rebuked the 'practice of carving up the populations of Europe as if they were cheeses,' and who slowly and arduously established the claims of national independence. When the Powers at Vienna punished France with one hand, with the other they restored the communities which they professed to liberate to a despotism more oppressive than anything they had suffered from Napoleon. But their plans have not outlived two generations; the victims of their benevolent dispositions have survived to rearrange Europe. Greece, Italy, Hungary, and the Balkan States—creations of the silent forces which confound the wisdom of Chancellors—have proved that the battle is not always to the strong. The century which produced Metternich, Bismarck, and Disraeli redeemed itself in the careers of Kossuth, Mazzini, and Gladstone; and the men to whom England owes

COLONIAL AND FOREIGN POLICY

it that she looks back with pride to the part she has played in those events were inspired by no other faith than that for which the insolent conceit of to-day is only concerned to find a contemptuous epigram or a decent cenotaph.

The Liberals who made the foreign policy of England during a great part of the century, and whose doctrines, as we believe, supply the true solution of our modern problems, were distinguished by three great principles. They believed in morality between nations, they respected and cherished the best instincts of a true nationalism, and they held that England could not cut herself off from the highest interests of Europe. Each of these principles is attacked by Imperialism.

In the long controversy between the friends and the enemies of international morality, the voice of Liberalism, through Gladstone as through Fox, denied that self-interest was the only law in high politics. Disraeli's Oriental trickery and the unscrupulous materialism of the law-breaker Bismarck were alike abhorrent to Mr. Gladstone. He recognised one code of honour for nations and for men. Contracts, treaties, and conventions were just as binding on statesmen as on private citizens. And this simple morality inspired Mr. Gladstone's nationalism. His instincts were not those of a sickly, still less those of a corrupt cosmopolitanism. A scrupulous regard for the honour of England, a special pride in what is

LIBERALISM AND THE EMPIRE

individual in her civilization, a care for her best traditions, a strenuous resistance to any proposals involving discredit to her good name, these were united in Mr. Gladstone with a strict respect for the right of national civilizations to maintain and express themselves, and a warm and effective sympathy with struggles towards national freedom.

This nationalist impulse was never lacking in Liberal statesmen. Fox denounced the partition of Poland in an indifferent Parliament. Byron died on the battlefield for Greece. Navarino made Canning famous. Palmerston himself, brawler as he was, half redeemed his long hours of bombastic passion over Don Pacifico's broken bedstead and his continual and ridiculous provocations to foreign Powers by a generous support of the cause of independence in Belgium and Italy. Mr. Gladstone boldly followed this principle in his actual policy as well as in his judgment of European affairs. The retrocession of the Ionian Islands and of the Transvaal, no part of a clumsy bargain, like the cession of Heligoland, were tributes to this ideal, not less genuine, and in one case far more heroic, than the welcome which English Liberalism gave to the victories of Hungary, of Italy, and of the European subjects of the Porte. His last political action was to appeal to his countrymen in the teeth of the chief London Liberal newspaper to befriend the causes of Armenia and the Cretans. And there is no European people which has fought, whether with hope or in despair, for its freedom that has not given to Mr. Gladstone's memory the special honours reserved for its national heroes.

But Mr. Gladstone's sense of nationalism did not merely govern his actions; it created the atmosphere in which he thought and spoke. The equality of nations he described as the greatest principle of all in foreign policy—'the sound and sacred principle that Christendom is formed of a band of nations who are united to one another in the bonds of right; they are without distinction of great and small; there is an absolute equality between them. The same sacredness defends the narrow limits of Belgium as attaches to the extended frontiers of Germany or Russia or France. I hold that he who by act or word brings that principle into peril or disparagement, however honest his intentions may be, places himself in the position of one inflicting injury upon his own country and endangering the peace and all the most fundamental interests of Christian society."

It was this doctrine of the equality of nations that Mr. Gladstone invoked against the self-sufficient arrogance of insularity. He held that a statesman owed to the dignity of his own nation a polite and temperate bearing towards other peoples. There are some men who treat all their neighbours with an impartial insolence, and then flatter themselves on their republican manners, a perversion of the uniform courtesy which the character implies. Mr. Gladstone did not so understand the equality of nations as to hector and insult them all alike; rather he believed that it is possible to behave like a gentleman in international as in private affairs. He disliked, as not less undignified than offensive, the diplomacy of which it may be said that its bark is generally worse than its bite. Above all, he hated the doctrine that England's greatness exempted her from the obligations which less favoured nations were expected to acknowledge — 'an untrue, arrogant, and dangerous assumption that we were entitled to assume for ourselves some dignity which we should also be entitled to withhold from others, and to claim on our own part authority to do things which we would not permit to be done by others.' With this strenuous and urbane sense of nationalism, Mr. Gladstone combined a keen appreciation of the position which England occupies in the scheme of European civilization. Unlike certain statesmen of modern times who, in their haste to conquer maps or extinguish nationalities in the Dark Continent, repudiate all responsibilities to the general system of European rights, Mr. Gladstone was proud that England had a share in the civilization of Western Europe, and that she had used her influence effectively to champion or safeguard the rights of nationality. He believed that the mutual affinities of the Liberalism of England, France, and

COLONIAL AND FOREIGN POLICY

Italy were not to be lightly sacrificed to individual rapacity. England was in his eyes a European Power. He had no sympathy with a policy which was always taking away the breath of Europe by some clever surprise. To deliberate foreign opinion he was not indifferent,[1] though he never made the mistake of reading the sentiments of the peoples in the organs of financial rings. It could not be said of a statesman who refused to purchase the favour of Bismarck by condoning the seizures of Alsace-Lorraine or Schleswig-Holstein that he allowed his course to be shaped and bent by every breath of prejudice or ill-will abroad. He was ready, if necessary, to run some risks in the cause of national freedom. Fear of Europe, he believed, should not paralyze the generosity of individual Powers; but a sense of duty to Europe should regulate their selfish ambitions. And England

---

[1] 'Lastly, there is also an appeal from the people of England to the general sentiment of the civilized world, and I for my part am of opinion that England will stand shorn of a chief part of her glory and her pride if she should be found separating herself, through the policy she pursues abroad, from the moral support which the convictions of mankind afford; if the day shall come when she may continue to excite the wonder and fear of other nations, but in which she shall have no part in their affection and regard. Let us recognise, and recognise with frankness, the equality of the weak with the strong, the principles of brotherhood among nations, and of their sacred independence.'—Debate on the Don Pacifico incident.

in particular owed it to her own history that she should not renounce all respect for the solidarity of that western civilization which her wisest statesmen had done so much to create.

None of these Liberal principles are to be found in the new ideal of national conduct and the new moral canon presented by Imperialism. The moral syllogism which it applies to politics runs thus: The British Empire is the greatest blessing known to mankind. Whatever helps to extend that Empire is good. Therefore, although a particular course of action may be immoral, in the sense that it is a breach of faith, or that it is an attack upon national rights, or that it implies violence, it becomes not merely innocent, but positively virtuous, if it helps to extend the Empire.

The merits of a particular quarrel are irrelevant if your ultimate victory is to increase the happiness of mankind; or acts which you would condemn as barbarous in any other circumstances, you must condone if they are incidents of expansion.

Thus stated, the apology for aggression looks a little crude. But will anyone deny that it represents substantially the train of reasoning which applauded, or at least forgave, the Jameson Raid, or the strain put upon the construction of the conventions by Mr. Chamberlain and the *Times?* But the contrast between the Liberal and the Imperialist position might be put in another form: The

COLONIAL AND FOREIGN POLICY

Liberal believes that the greatness of the British Empire imposes a special obligation to act with self-control and moderation; the Imperialist sees in it an authority for disregarding the restraints which he would recognise as binding on a State less powerful and less beneficent. There are certain things, argues the Liberal, which our very strength makes it at once impolitic and unchivalrous for the British Empire to do. Great Britain's position is such, argues the Imperialist, that she must not be held to her word, or hampered by conventions like other people; she acts as the right hand of Providence in regenerating the world, and no technical obstacles must be allowed to interfere with her mission of carrying from continent to continent the energies of a just and sublime civilization, the art of a new and diviner governance. And the glamour of science is thrown over immorality as well as the glamour of romance. The great biological discoveries of the century supply an analogy which, curiously enough, is pressed into the service of the Imperialist propaganda by men who never accepted the discoveries themselves. Pulpits which shrieked against Darwin are now twittering with pseudo-Darwinisms. The survival of the fittest, the struggles of conflicting civilizations, the God-given rule of the perfection of type by the murder of nations—these are the recognised commonplaces of theologians who, though they would not accept the monkey as the type of undeveloped man, are tumbling over each other in their haste to acclaim the tiger or the wild cat as the image of his maturity.

For one of the most noticeable features of the modern crisis is the action of the ecclesiastical conscience. Whilst Mr. Herbert Spencer follows Voltaire in denouncing aggression, our clergy is, for the most part, content to fill the part of the French Archbishops whom Voltaire so roundly attacked for promising their benisons to popular wars.[1] And the first thing that strikes us is the curious paradox: that whilst our divines who rejected biological evolution accept a certain moral parallel which has been drawn from it, the scientific men who taught and developed the first regard the second as fundamentally unscientific and false. Mr. Huxley, in his Romanes Lecture at Oxford, sounded a note of warning against this kind of loose reasoning.

The Bishops called the biologists heretics in religion, and as soon as they begin to adapt the scientific discoveries of the biologists to morals, they are found by the biologist to be themselves heretics in science. And if we look a little closer, the reason is at once apparent. The men who never accepted the scientific system are scarcely our safest guides when it is our business to draw moral conclusions

[1] Mr. Morley in his great speech at Oxford described 'pulpit militarism' as perhaps the worst of all the symptoms of retrograde humour in the community.—See *Manchester Guardian*, June 11, 1900.

COLONIAL AND FOREIGN POLICY

from it. For instead of applying the system in the spirit and with the precision of its masters, they borrow a few of its exoteric expressions in order to add a tinsel of scientific decoration to the crude form of a vulgar morality which, stripped of this meretricious apparel, scarcely differs from the morality of the savage. They have forgotten that the survival of the fittest applies not only to the combatants in the struggle, but to the struggle itself. They commit, in consequence, a stupendous anachronism. For the men of science argue that, as the result of generations of evolution, mankind has now reached a plane on which the struggle is no longer military. One form of competition has supplanted another, and war is no longer the normal type. Every individual becomes more and more dependent both for his prosperity and for his very existence on the goodwill of the community, and every community becomes more and more dependent on the goodwill of mankind. The Bishops—and they must be taken in this relation to represent the whole class of bloodthirsty divines, not, of course, divines in general—are, as is perhaps not surprising, a full stage behind the men of science, and when they talk of conflicting types of civilization, they imagine not a competition in industry, in commerce, in spreading enlightened notions, in distributing knowledge more widely, and in extending a respect for humane and honourable ideas, but a competition with Mausers, with Maxims, and with

LIBERALISM AND THE EMPIRE

lyddite. The highest type of civilization is to prevail —yes, but only by borrowing the weapons of an earlier stage of human development. Society is to advance by taking a long stride backwards. Whereas Mr. Herbert Spencer thinks that all has been gained from war (in the matter of organizing types) which war has to give, Bishops look to war as a means of spreading Christianity. And the nation is encouraged to abandon the Christian virtues of pity and moderation, and to adopt from science, not tolerance, reasonableness, and a liberal mind, but only an analogy which science has itself rejected.

Is it possible to imagine a compromise between religion and science which could more gratuitously neutralize the advantages of both, than one in which Christianity sacrifices what would seem to be essential to its morality in exchange for something which is not science at all?

It is the major premiss of the Imperialist argument that British civilization is the best in the world. If this only meant that the British genius is more adapted than any other to success in certain great fields of energy, and that an Englishman may point with pride to a long series of great and honourable triumphs in those fields, there would be nothing to complain of in our national habit of self-confidence, except that the manner of its expression is sometimes in rather odious taste. But in the mouth of the Imperialist it means a great deal more.

COLONIAL AND FOREIGN POLICY

The moral hegemony of the world which we have undertaken—we are ready to share it with America when she behaves herself to our satisfaction or when Europe is more than usually insolent—might be expected to imply that our conduct and our influence should act as a beneficent example upon other States. The phrase is that we are the schoolmasters of Europe. To justify the claim the Imperialist points to the open door in our possessions, to the satisfactory commercial principles on which we run our dependencies, to the economies and stability of our administration. Nobody doubts that the world would gain from the general adoption of our policy of Free Trade, if only because amongst other things which some of our Imperialists propose to sacrifice to their enthusiasms is Free Trade itself. But the analogy from the schoolmasters is carried a great deal further. As schoolmasters we are told that we stand outside the discipline of the school. Mr. Bryce has shown that during the negotiations with the Transvaal Government we contrived to provoke war before we had discovered a *casus belli*. It is not pretended that these negotiations would have been so conducted if we had been dealing with a Great Power, or, indeed, if we had known the strength of the Transvaal. In other words, we were taking advantage of our physical superiority. And how is that course of action defended? By reminding ourselves of our missionary character! By recalling all the blessings which the world will reap from the extension of our Empire! But what is the effect of this spectacle upon our pupils? Are those nations which have been invited to sit at our feet going to learn from this example to abandon the vices of chicanery, sharp practice, and intrigue? And if it is retorted that no other State in Europe would have shown a more scrupulous respect for international law, the whole case is abandoned, for the more Europe requires to be morally elevated the more obligatory the responsibility of the nation which has assumed that office.

There is a very practical manner in which this talk of our Imperial mission to make mankind happy and free acts upon Europe to the deterioration rather than the advancement of humanity. If we welcome our manifest destiny to absorb territory and to govern the affairs of the universe, the nations whose manifest destiny it is to see their territory absorbed and their affairs governed by ourselves have less reason to be satisfied with their lot.

Imperium et Libertas is no new watchword. It is more than twenty years old, and when it was invented Mr. Gladstone showed that a proclamation which meant 'Liberty for ourselves, and Empire over the rest of mankind,' was a danger signal to humanity.

'If one thing more than another has been detestable in Europe, it has been the appearance upon the stage from time to time of men who, even in the times of Christian civilization, have been thought to aim at universal dominion. It was this aggressive disposition on the part of Louis XIV., King of France, that led your forefathers freely to spend their blood and treasure in a cause not immediately their own, and to struggle against the method of policy which, having Paris for its centre, seemed to aim at a universal monarchy. It was the very same thing a century and a half later which was the charge launched—and justly launched—against Napoleon, that under his dominion France was not content even with her extended limits, but Germany and Italy and Spain, apparently without any limit to this pestilent and pernicious process, were to be brought under the dominion or influence of France, and national equality was to be trampled under foot, and national rights denied. For that reason England in the struggle almost exhausted herself, greatly impoverished her people, brought upon herself and Scotland too the consequences of a debt that nearly crushed their energies, and poured forth their best blood without limit in order to resist and put down these intolerable pretensions.'—Third Midlothian speech.

The case of Napoleon is singularly relevant. As his unconquered armies swept through half of Europe, there was no country into which the son of the Revolution carried fire and sword in which he did not establish laws infinitely better than those which he abolished. If ever tyranny was redeemed by material improvement, it was a tyranny which awoke Europe from the slumber of medievalism. Habitually living in a false perspective, discovering another Waterloo in an engagement with undrilled Dervishes, recognising a Nelson and a Wellington in the Deweys and Kitcheners of modern warfare, our Imperialists can scarcely be so deceived by these optical illusions as to exaggerate the interval which they assume to separate English from other civilizations into the distance which divided the revolutionary from the feudal order. But Europe, and England most of all, refused to acquiesce on that account in Napoleon's aggression. And it is far more unreasonable to expect that nearly a century later Europe is going to acquiesce in our claim to be a law unto ourselves.

Englishmen ask themselves modestly, as they read translations from the Continental prints, why it is that Heaven has given these foreigners a double dose of the original sin of malice and uncharitableness towards their betters, as if the cause of that ill-will which broods over the Continent to-day were some inscrutable mystery. There are doubtless sections of Continental populations always ready to welcome our embarrassments. The envy and hatred which certain Englishmen cherish towards their neighbours are to be found in the sentiments of some of our neighbours towards ourselves—perhaps in greater degree on account of our prosperity and strength. But we cannot attribute to this cause the unanimity of Powers which agree in nothing except their unfriendliness towards us. And need we look very far for an adequate explanation? How did our Government keep the solemn promise which it made to the world that it would thoroughly and publicly investigate the Raid? Foreign opinion counts for nothing if you are a law to yourself. But is it surprising that a war with the Transvaal, four years after the Raid, is regarded as a repetition of that Raid; and that the Powers are restless and uneasy? We owe the black looks of Europe to the man who most conspicuously expresses the manner and professes the morality of Imperialism. There is not a nation which is not smarting under one of his insults. There is certainly not a statesman who would trust him. He refuses to clear his character of complicity in the Raid, and he gave a public testimonial to the chief member of the syndicate which organized that ignominious enterprise He is everywhere believed to have lent his sanction to the most flagrant outrage on public law in modern times—the invasion of a friendly State in the midst of profound peace. A disciple of Bismarck who has borrowed the morals without acquiring the power of his master, Mr. Chamberlain is judged by Europe to be unscrupulous and self-seeking, without being strong. And can a nation which has publicly idolized Mr. Rhodes, which tolerates Mr. Chamberlain in office, and which haughtily ignores the opinion of the civilized world[1]—can such a nation wonder that Europe is suspicious and resentful? Mr. Chamberlain wrote his despatches to President Kruger under the shadow of the Raid. It is under that shadow that he speaks, he treats, and he bargains; that he offers insults to one Power and adulation to another. As long as he remains a Minister this dark shadow overhangs the public honour of England and the public peace of Europe.

The new morality into which some of our professional moralists have imported a false flavour of naturalism is a matter of life and death to Englishmen, and especially to English Liberals. For if it be granted that it is only for the ultimate illumination of mankind that we are making this bonfire of our moral scruples, it is still pertinent to ask how much of our conscience is to survive. There are some who assume that the flames will only singe it. It is a dangerous optimism. 'If you wish to love mankind, you must not expect too much from them.' And after setting up two standards, one for conduct in Imperial affairs and the other for conduct in domestic affairs, it is asking a good deal of the rigour of human nature to expect that men will not come to apply the lower standard to both.

Mr. Herbert Spencer has indicated deductively,

[1] When this opinion was concerned with the domestic affairs of France, the *Times* described it as 'the voice of history.'

COLONIAL AND FOREIGN POLICY

and Mr. Morley has shown by positive illustration, that the vices of an aggressive spirit do not reserve themselves for display abroad, but cut inwards, sapping the vigour and the independence of States. The last few years have accumulated new and terrible examples. It is only by careful reflection that Englishmen will picture how much of their humanity, of their respect for truth, of their love of justice and fair-play they have already been called upon to sacrifice to this recrudescence of a Jesuitical spirit, which, when it showed itself in the service of religion, they were so quick to condemn as the invention of the devil. It is not too much to say of the Jameson Raid that it was unredeemed by the display of a single one of those qualities which appeal to the normal Englishman. There was not even personal courage on the field to convert what was burglary into the more romantic affair of the highwayman. There was not even honour among thieves. Mr. Rhodes was convicted of crimes not hitherto regarded as venial in public or private life, yet he received a welcome from London which would have been appropriate to a great national hero. He counts divines amongst his apologists, Court personages and an ex-Premier amongst his friends, the chief newspapers amongst his private organs, and the Poet Laureate is a kind of pocket Homer to his Achilles.

Mr. Chamberlain's dictatorship is another milestone on the long road of degradation of character. He lies under a grave charge, and a great part of the press affects surprise at the demand that a Minister of the Crown should clear his character. A chartered libertine in foreign politics, accustomed to break through all the recognised restraints of civilized Europe, a diplomatist who has strained the meaning of a treaty and committed the nation to an act which he had himself beforehand declared to be immoral, Mr. Chamberlain refuses to recognise what he owes to the honour of his country. And the Imperialist newspapers are just as contemptuous of the view that the public honour is concerned to acquit our Ministers of an offence against the law of nations. And yet there are people who think that an outlaw nation with high principles runs no risk of degenerating into a nation of outlaws with none, and that if in the name of civilization you habitually snap your fingers at public law, you are somewhere else than on the highway to moral anarchy.

If our new morality has obliged us to revise our notions of honour, how has it affected our humanity? Something more than the grease has been rubbed off that unctuous rectitude which was so obnoxious to the burly simplicity of Mr. Rhodes. It is true that we have lately heard a great deal from rather unexpected quarters of our duties to the black man in the Transvaal. But why is it only in the Transvaal

COLONIAL AND FOREIGN POLICY

that the black man has claims upon us? All President Kruger's genius for that form of satire which is generally known as cant has never invented anything quite so audacious as a humanity which owes nothing to our own black subjects, and acknowledges a debt to the black subjects of another State, reluctantly to be discharged by appropriating the State itself. Love your neighbour's black men as if they will one day be your own, and treat your own as if they belonged to anybody rather than to yourselves—this is the motto of Rhodesians who call the Boer a Pharisee. But I am not now concerned with the revolting hypocrisy with which a chivalrous protection for the weak is claimed as the object of this war by the organs and the admirers of the men who exhausted the resources without recognising the restraints of civilization in annihilating Mashonas, Matabeles, and Bechuanas, and who contemplated methods of exterminating niggers too revolting to describe. There is another moral to be drawn from our complacent indifference to Mr. Rhodes's conduct. The Matabele were first duped and cajoled into making concessions to the Goldfields Company, then deliberately provoked into war, and finally crushed with every circumstance of brutality and horror. Mr. Rhodes, after securing the transfer of British Bechuanaland to Cape Colony in 1895, made a slight disturbance the pretext for a great campaign, hunted, shot down, and starved out the Bechuana, and deported 2,000 of them to Capetown. The Chartered Company introduced, as Sir Richard Martin reported, a system of forced labour into Rhodesia. These things were done in the name of England. There are a good many Liberals who, at the risk of being sneered at by a British Proconsul as 'an anti-slavery faction,' believe that it is a much greater dishonour to England that she should allow her flag to fly over murder and treachery and pillage, than that she should refuse its shelter and protection to a motley group of marauding financiers, who measure civilization by their fortunes, and select their fatherland as other men select their banks. We would deliberately prefer that these territories should be left to unredeemed barbarism rather than capture them for civilization under a black flag. But how many Englishmen, in ordinary life humane and civilized, regard all these as the inevitable incidents of expansion! The youth who 'never missed seeing a nigger shot in Buluwayo' confessed that he could never have brought himself to watch a man hanged in England. Where is this brutalizing development to end?

Let a sane Englishman sit down and study carefully the language, the correspondence, the pictures, which figure in the daily press on the subject of the present war, the toys which are sold in our streets, and then ask himself whether there is not very prevalent in polite England an idea of pleasure which differs not much from that of the savage. We have stood so much that it is difficult to know whether there is anything at which we should turn squeamish. It is no wonder that Earl Grey, having found no limits to our endurance, talks openly of the necessity of slavery. He recognises with complacency that in civilizing the world we are in danger of relapsing into barbarism, and that we are purchasing the morality of Africa at the price of our own.

In the moral revolution which has made the Imperialist, all sense of nationality has perished. An attachment to national tradition, a scrupulous jealousy for the honour of your country, a desire to express and preserve her individuality, the qualities which make up the temperament of nationalism, find no place in the psychology of the megalomaniac. There is nothing distinctively English in aggression. The notion that because England has certain special aptitudes for organization the mere accumulation of administrative responsibilities and tropical deserts satisfies and expresses her aspirations is grotesquely inadequate.

The use of the term Anglo-Saxon in modern journalism symbolizes fitly the desertion of the old national basis of unity. As a pseudo-scientific name for the British-born inhabitants of the southern, eastern, and central parts of our island, considered in their racial origin, 'Anglo-Saxon' might pass muster. But when it was made to include not only

LIBERALISM AND THE EMPIRE

the whole population of the British Isles—Ireland, the Scottish Highlands, Wales, the West Country and the Great Wen with its swarm of metics—not only our colonies and our dependencies, but the United States of North America themselves—the word escaped ridicule by evading definition. It is not wonderful that when our patriots wanted a common name for this motley and fortuitous conglomeration, the word English should have stuck in their mouths; it is unimaginable that they should have chosen for so illimitable a category a denomination more restricted still. But let the word remain. Let us reserve the old name English to designate the vital and racy qualities of our nation; and let Anglo-Saxon be the glorious epithet of their deformity and their tumefaction for ever.

The new enthusiasm sacrifices much that is preeminently English for something which is not English at all. The Imperialist cares nothing about our tradition of free speech. He has chosen to imitate in South Africa the methods of repressive governments rather than to exhibit our historical tolerance of racial diversities. And the men whose ideal is a strenuous, virile, self-respecting, and honourable England are called 'Little Englanders' by a party which clamours for a tumid, plethoric, dissipated England, big at the expense of her greatness, sacrificing for mere territory the prizes of her history, with no memory for her traditions—a conscienceless

COLONIAL AND FOREIGN POLICY

England with a lumbering, topheavy body and with feet of clay. Better a 'little England' than an England swollen and bloated out of recognition. For what is the Imperialist's notion of England's honour? Four years ago we were told that we could only stand idly by whilst the Sultan massacred in thousands a community which we were bound by treaty to protect. Two years ago Russia ordered us to withdraw our ships from Port Arthur, and the Government complied. The indignity was not redeemed by petulant assertions after our retreat that our ships had the best of rights to be there. During the South African War the German Government presented certain demands in its most peremptory manner, and our Government first obeyed and then complained. Recall our action on these occasions and then recollect the exuberant enthusiasm with which certain of our chief papers and politicians adjured the greatest of Empires to make war upon a couple of tiny Republics with a united peasant population comparable to that of a respectable English borough—a romantic enterprise to which was to be summoned, as though to a crusade, the valour of her colonies in all the distant corners of the world. The Imperialist and the Anglophobe meet in a common misconception of England's character—' Parcere superbis et debellare subjectos.'

Caring little for our national traditions, our new Imperialists care still less for the claims of

LIBERALISM AND THE EMPIRE

national freedom elsewhere. Imperialism finds its triumphs in the sable funerals of nationalities. If Mr. Rudyard Kipling adds to the moral imagination of a savage any more precise enthusiasm of his own, it may be said of him that he is never happy unless he is in at the death of nations. What has become of nationalism as an inspiring or as a restraining influence upon English politics during the last four years? During the dispute and the war between Greece and Turkey our fleet, which every Englishman has sometime called the 'mistress of the sea,' was degraded to the service of the German Emperor's ambitions. Treaty-pledges, the indefeasible claims of a population struggling to be free, the arguments based on moral obligations, counted for nothing in the eyes of men who were all for circumspection and prudence when their honour called for action, as they were all for rashness and haste when duty demanded self-restraint. The strong popular impulses in England, France, and Italy were wasted by an irresolute and indecisive policy, and all the Liberalism of Europe was impotent to strike a blow or to speak a word for freedom.

These things were bad enough. The century which has been called by an eminent French writer[1] the

[1] M. Brunetière in the *Quarterly Review*, April, 1900. An illustration of the growth of the sentiment in the century may be noticed in the horror provoked by the violation of the feelings of a population in the seizure of Alsace Lorraine.

COLONIAL AND FOREIGN POLICY

century of the renaissance of nationalities was about to close in the temporary eclipse of the great principle which had made it famous. Its sun was to set on the triumphs of the Porte, on the extinction of the constitution of Finland, on the great Powers scrambling for territory, on England careless of all the causes she had made her own. But there is something yet more to be dreaded than that mortal fatigue against which Mr. Morley once warned his countrymen. Worse than all the disappointments of the last few years is the blight which has been cast over South Africa by the twin curses of Imperialism and avarice; and the century closes upon an England not merely indifferent to the crimes of others, but guilty herself of a crime against nationality.

It rarely happens that such opportunities are presented to the imagination of a people as that offered to England in the summer of 1899. The principle of nationalism, which alone protects civilization from the barbarous tyranny known as the right of the stronger, had indisputably lost ground in Europe and America. England held a tiny community in the hollow of her hand. All that was corrupt in her society called upon the Government to crush it. It was generally believed that she had but to move her little finger and the Transvaal was doomed. Two things stood between her and that act. The one was her pledged word; the other her respect for nationality. Self-restraint at that moment would have taught the world that England still cherished the moral principle which had been treated with scant respect during the last few years, and that her professions at the Hague were not all polite formalities. Then was the moment to play the schoolmaster. The opportunity was lost. An Imperialism which places under a ban the patriotism of every other nation had no difficulty in discovering pretexts for aggression. It was argued that a great democratic people was in honour bound to overthrow the domestic system of another nation for the benefit of unenfranchised immigrants. We were reminded that the civilization of the Boers was out of date, as if that had anything to do with the morality of war. We were invited to remember the primitive methods of their agriculture, the un-English forms of their government, the convenience of the Imperial power, the affront put upon our dignity by the hesitation of an old man to concede the full franchise to a turbulent population of aliens. For those who do not judge every civilization by its drainage system, there were stories of atrocities and outrage. Even the Jameson Raid was invoked, not to illustrate Mr. Rhodes's character, but to show that Englishmen were in danger of sharing the fate of the Armenians. And the result of all this misrepresentation and immoral doctrine is that we find ourselves at this moment on the verge of a deed for which no parallel can be found since Poland was distributed more than a century ago amongst the crowned ruffians of that day. Our action is justified by the plea that if we are taking their flag from the Boers with one hand, we are giving them good government with the other, which is very much what Catherine and her royal accomplice said about Poland.

Mr. Chamberlain has told us that annexation is, after all, not such a very terrible calamity for the Boers—a remark which illustrates the man and his times. To a certain order of temperament all life is made up of good municipal systems; to a certain temperament it is plain that if you promise a community the right to vote some day at its local elections, it has no reason to complain of the loss of its flag. And the times and circumstances of the eclipse of our traditional regard for nationality are significant. The South African War marks the triumph of a set of financiers whose kind is to be found not in South Africa only. Having no patriotism of their own, they make it their business to exploit the patriotism of others. Mr. Hobson has described their intrigues, their manipulation of the press, their insidious concentration of political power.[1] Their avarice has never been checked by any reverence for the flag or the honour of England, and it is, perhaps, not surprising they have had no scruples in overturning traditions in which they have themselves no part or lot.

[1] 'The War in South Africa.'

LIBERALISM AND THE EMPIRE

Their sordid materialism was unable to imagine a love of country which would take the field against overwhelming odds. Mr. Rhodes regards our flag as a commercial asset. It is no wonder he thought four years ago that a handful of irregulars could seize the Transvaal, and last year that an army division would reduce Pretoria before Christmas, for he knew nothing of the divine infatuation which makes men give their blood for their country, or he fancied that the day of those simple follies and old-world heroisms had gone by, superseded by the civilization of De Beers. This new order, which threatens the peace of the world and corrupts every national civilization, finds an easy prey in a community careless of all moral ideals. And the chief obstacle to its ambition is just the nationalist spirit which Imperialism seeks to extinguish.

It is urged that if our Imperialist masters have renounced moral principles and all respect for nationality, they are in spite of that, or indeed because of that, good men of affairs, in whose hands the interests of the Empire are safe, and who have shown by their diplomacy that they will stand no nonsense. Let us test by this criterion the proceedings of the last four years. It was complained of a great philosopher that he made revolution the diet instead of the medicine of States. Of Mr. Chamberlain it may be said that he finds the ordinary fare of his diplomacy in extemporized crises and loaded ulti-

COLONIAL AND FOREIGN POLICY

matums, the desperate remedies of saner men. And it is not only our rivals who have been bewildered by his escapades. If Englishmen have been unable during the last few years to contemplate the Empire except in a series of dissolving views, distracted like children by each new fantasy, what of their rulers? We have seen Mr. Chamberlain one day at the throat of Europe; the next at the feet of Germany. So fickle and so fleeting have been our admirations and our vanities that those who wished to be quite up-to-date and orthodox in their patriotism have been uncertain at any given moment whether a contemptuous detachment,[1] a jumble of all things Saxon,[2] or a condominium of the English-speaking races[3] might be the latest fashion amongst their masters.

Mr. Chamberlain himself changes moods within a few hours. In the same speech in the middle of which he offered our hand to Germany, he told Europe, in his peroration, that England and America divided all that there was of the higher civilization and humanitarian sentiment in mankind.[4] Is it surprising that a whirl of volatile enthusiasms have chased each other through the press? Day-dreams of an all-powerful England, regarding with an Olympian indifference the trivial jealousies of Europe, have been followed by nightmares of bristling con-

---

[1] Mr. Goschen, 1896. [2] Mr. Chamberlain, 1898.
[3] Mr. Chamberlain, *passim*. [4] Birmingham, 1898.

LIBERALISM AND THE EMPIRE

spiracies. The mirage of a *pax Britannica*[1] lifted from our view, to disclose the terrifying portents of Armageddon.[2] When we claimed the right to govern the world, inferior nations displayed an intelligible if a childish petulance. What we lost in dignity by prostrating ourselves before Germany we did not gain in popularity by explaining that it was only the incurable immorality of France and Russia that had forced us into that unnatural posture. Whatever the mood of the moment, we have contrived so to indulge it as to insult our neighbours and increase our military expenditure.

Does anyone pretend that we reaped any solid benefit out of the mortifications, the risks, and the vagaries of our Chinese policy? Our Ministers apparently never foresaw that Germany's seizure of Kiao Chou would lead to a general scramble, and in spite of Russia's direct representations, they took no precautions and prepared no policy. We adopted a resolution declaring that the maintenance of the integrity of China was all-important. At that moment we had already connived at Germany's seizure of one port, and before many months had passed we had ourselves occupied another. We contrived in a manner and degree almost unparalleled to combine all the disadvantages of weakness and violence. Our Ministers prefaced their concessions to Russia with threats, and followed

[1] Lord Curzon, 1895. [2] Mr. Chamberlain, 1898.

them with insults. When Russia seized Port Arthur Lord Salisbury pitied her folly, and Mr. Chamberlain cursed her double-dealing. Mr. Chamberlain said we had been swindled; Lord Salisbury thought we had got the best of the bargain, whilst the country followed in bewilderment the Government's zigzag career and conflicting apologies. Mr. Morley, discussing these strange contradictions, illustrated very happily the incongruous elements of the Cabinet:

"Lord Salisbury had said that Russia had made a great mistake in her own interests, and that she had committed an unfortunate blunder in taking Port Arthur. He had a great admiration for philosophy, but Lord Salisbury had a colleague who had got a little more of old Adam in him—a colleague of a more primitive and elementary moral build than the Premier —and that colleague had relieved his feelings by a good natural outburst of railing and swearing. He was referring to a speech made by the Colonial Minister at Birmingham. There had been conjunctions in our history which needed a great war Minister, and there had been conjunctions which needed a great peace Minister. Chatham was a war Minister, Walpole was a peace Minister. But what they never wanted was a Minister half Chatham and half Walpole. They never wanted a Minister as Walpole in the morning and Chatham in the afternoon. They might still have in Yorkshire that old barometer or weather-gauge on which when fine the woman came out, and when stormy the man. But what a maddening weather-gauge was ours, when before the prudent Walpole had had time to go in at his peaceful door out popped Chatham—not life-size—storming and threatening."[1]

On one side men argued in favour of resisting Russia's demands by force, on the other in favour of effecting an understanding with Russia. Our Ministers let Russia have her way, and yet contrived to make her as hostile as if we had withstood her. And everyone knows that the net result of a series of diplomatic somersaults in the Far East was to leave Russia stronger than ever in China. We waited to open up direct negotiations with Russia until we had already discredited our authority by withdrawing our ships from Port Arthur at her dictation. And as if these reverses were not enough, we plunged into a war in South Africa, which obliged us to leave Russia a free hand in China, allowing ourselves to be drawn into a quarrel fomented for their own purposes by a group of millionaires, out of which the nation as a whole never stood to reap anything but disaster.

Liberalism and Imperialism differ in their morals, their manners, and their ideals. Let us illustrate the contrast by two final examples. Liberalism was a peaceful influence; Imperialism means war, and war for ignoble purposes. Cobden and Bright never dictated the foreign policy of an English Government, but they taught England two great doctrines:

[1] Mr. Morley at Leeds, June 8, 1898.

COLONIAL AND FOREIGN POLICY

the first the doctrine of non-intervention in the domestic affairs of another nation; the second the doctrine that commerce flourishes on peace and international goodwill. The pretensions of a creed which makes interference a virtue if English interests, or the interests of Englishmen, naturalized or otherwise, are in some mysterious way to be advanced, and which teaches the ridiculous fallacy that war is in the interest of trade, are a constant menace to the peace of the world. Again, the intolerance of the Imperialist exhibits itself most conspicuously in his attitude to a country which has always attracted the special friendship of Liberals.

For the Liberals of this century the solidarity of Western civilization has meant the triumphs and the progress of humane impulses due to the interaction of Liberal opinion in the two chief Liberalizing nations. And it is with good reason that they have so regarded the relations of the two countries, and that Fox, Byron, Peel, Cobden, Mr. Gladstone,[1] Mr. Morley,[2] and Sir Henry Campbell-Bannerman, have all extended to

[1] 'Deeply impressed, as we ever have been, with the value and importance, not only of friendly relations, but even of something in the nature of a special amity between France and our own country.'—'Gleanings,' vol. iv., p. 214.

[2] See Mr. Morley's speech at Leicester, 1898: 'Both together surpassing all the nations in the world besides in what they have done for human freedom and enlightenment.' To this list of Liberal statesmen must be added a great writer who is also a great Liberal—Mr. George Meredith.

LIBERALISM AND THE EMPIRE

France the sympathy and admiration which partnership in great civilizing ideas fosters and develops.

Sir Spencer Walpole in his 'History of England from 1815' enumerates thirteen reforms[1] to illustrate the growth of more beneficent and kindlier sentiments in the forty years following the overthrow of Napoleon. In the case of more than half of these reforms the example was set by France, and in the case of the rest the example was set by England. The first effect of the French Revolution was to throw back the energies of reform in England, but no society regenerated by that great tumultuous shock, which was to give to Europe a new face and a new conscience, owes quite so much to France as the nation which has travelled farthest along the road to her distant ideals.

But this historical association and this community of ideas count for nothing to our modern Imperialists.

The desire to mortify France by making the withdrawal of the French Government from an untenable position at Fashoda as difficult as possible, the unrestrained abuse of France and everything French during the Dreyfus affair, were symptoms of that

[1] Abolition of slavery. Regulation of female and child labour. Limitation of capital punishment. Reform of penal system. Abolition of cruel punishments. Abolition of imprisonment for debt. Suppression of duelling. Suspension of impressment. Limitation of flogging in the army. Prohibition of cruel sports. Punishment of cruelty to animals. More humane treatment of lunatics. Employment of anæsthetics.

COLONIAL AND FOREIGN POLICY

mingled contempt and dislike which they cherish towards our great neighbour. Mr. Chamberlain has never concealed his hatred of France. He wished for war over West Africa as well as over the Soudan; he addressed an insolent reprimand to her at Leicester; alone of all our public men he was guilty of the grave irregularity of commenting upon a case awaiting trial in that country.

And of all the effects of that intolerance which regards every diversity of religion, of polity, as an eyesore, which sees a moribund civilization in every civilization not immediately intelligible or sympathetic to our own, which feeds itself on a boasted ignorance,[1] and takes pride in its rigid Procrustean measurements of every nation by our own standard, none is so disastrous as the alienation of two peoples whose co-operation has done so much for freedom in Europe, and in whose friendship the interests of Europe and of humanity are so peculiarly involved.

The objection is brought against us to-day, as it was brought against Liberals in the past, that we are indifferent to the interests of the Empire. Mr. Gladstone had to answer the accusation in

[1] Mr. Chamberlain, of course, provides the most frequent illustrations; but it would be unjust to Captain Hedworth Lambton to ignore a passage in his speech to the Anglo-African writers, which bids fair to become a *locus classicus*. Captain Lambton said that no one who didn't understand English knew what liberty meant, and that it was only England and America who practised freedom.

LIBERALISM AND THE EMPIRE

1881: 'While we are opposed to Imperialism, we are devoted to the Empire, and we who are now in Government as your agents will, to the best and utmost and latest of our power, whilst studying peace with all the world, endeavour to persuade men into the observance of the laws of justice and equity.'

Mr. Gladstone never allowed this cheap sneer to affect his conduct. Take his words when he was defending the retrocession of the Transvaal:

'We have not been afraid of reproach at home, as we have not been afraid of calumny in the colonies, on account of the over-indulgence which, as was said, we extended to the Boers of the Transvaal. . . . It is a common reproach against us, the Liberals of England, that we are indifferent to the greatness of the Empire. One thing I will say: I hope the Liberals of England will never seek to consolidate the Empire by ministering to the interests of class instead of the public. And I hope they will never seek to extend the Empire by either violently wresting or fraudulently obtaining the territories of other people.'

It would hardly have seemed necessary to prove that the author of the Midlothian speeches disliked Imperialism. But as an important newspaper has lately begun to claim for its own views on South African policy the posthumous support of the great statesman whose last efforts in the cause of freedom in Europe it so indefatigably and persistently withstood, I may be excused for examining in some little

COLONIAL AND FOREIGN POLICY

detail the evidence the *Daily News* has to submit in defence of its interesting and original interpretation of Mr. Gladstone's attitude.

Here is the quotation from Mr. Gladstone's speech which is most frequently offered to us: 'I believe that we are all united—indeed, it would be most unnatural if we were not—in a fond attachment, perhaps in something of a proud attachment, to the great country to which we belong—to this great Empire, which has committed to it a trust and a function given from Providence as special and as remarkable as ever was entrusted to any portion of the family of man. Gentlemen, when I speak of that trust and that function I feel that words fail me: I cannot tell you what I think of the nobleness of the inheritance that has descended upon us, of the sacredness of the duty of maintaining it. I will not condescend to make it a part of controversial politics. It is a part of my being, of my flesh and blood, of my heart and soul. For those ends I have laboured through my youth and manhood till my hairs are gray. In that faith and practice I have lived; in that faith and practice I will die.'

The conclusion which the *Daily News* draws from this passage is that Mr. Gladstone must be classed with the Liberal Imperialists, the politicians who support the present war. But read the passage immediately before this selection:

'I have spoken, and I must speak in very strong

LIBERALISM AND THE EMPIRE

terms indeed, of the acts done by my opponents, but I will never ascribe those acts to base motives. I will never say they do them from vindictiveness; I will never say they do them from passion; I will never say they do them from a sordid love of office. I have no right to use such words; I have no right to entertain such sentiments; I repudiate and abjure them. I give them credit for patriotic motives; I give them credit for those patriotic motives which are so incessantly and gratuitously denied to us.'

Mr. Gladstone was explaining that he would never condescend to impeach the patriotism of the men who called him by opprobrious names because he differed from them on foreign policy. And what was it of which he had spoken 'in very strong terms indeed'? It was the entire foreign policy of Lord Beaconsfield's Ministry; the Imperialism of his own generation. In the course of his Midlothian campaign he attacked Lord Beaconsfield's Turkish policy; he attacked the Afghan War and he attacked the annexation of the Transvaal. In other words, Mr. Gladstone, in a speech in which he had relentlessly assailed the Government of his day, affirmed that he would never make the sacredness of the duty of maintaining our noble inheritance a part of controversial politics. The *Daily News*, isolating his peroration, concludes that he would have acquiesced in the aggressions of modern Imperialism. To anyone reading the passage in its context, the

COLONIAL AND FOREIGN POLICY

conclusion to be drawn is obviously that Mr. Gladstone would have held that in attacking the Imperialism of to-day no Liberal was open to the accusation of a lack of 'proud attachment to the Great Empire.' When read with its context the passage is a rebuke to the men and newspapers who inflame party controversy by impugning the patriotism of their opponents. The *Daily News* and Sir Henry Fowler seriously argue that it is a rebuke to the men and newspapers who criticise the foreign policy of the Government of the day—a rebuke from the statesman who was at that very moment engaged in one of the fiercest campaigns ever waged against an aggressive Ministry. And to show finally Mr. Gladstone's whole-hearted dislike for the thing as well as the word Imperialism, let us recall his own statement of his principles of foreign policy:

'I first give you what I think the right principles of foreign policy. The first thing is to foster the strength of the Empire by just legislation and economy at home, thereby producing two of the great elements of national power—namely, wealth, which is a physical element, and union and contentment, which are moral elements—and to reserve the strength of the Empire, to reserve the expenditure of that strength, for great and worthy occasions abroad. Here is my first principle of foreign policy: Good government at home. My second principle of foreign policy is this: That its aim ought to be to preserve to the nations of the world—and especially were it but for shame when we recollect the sacred name we bear as Christians, especially to the Christian nations of the world—the blessings of peace. That is my second principle.

'My third principle is this: Even when you do a good thing, you may do it in so bad a way that you may entirely spoil the beneficial effect; and if we were to make ourselves the apostles of peace in the sense of conveying to the minds of other nations that we thought ourselves more entitled to an opinion on that subject than they are, or to deny their rights— well, very likely we should destroy the whole value of our doctrines. In my opinion the third sound principle is this: To strive to cultivate and maintain —ay, to the very uttermost—what is called the Concert of Europe, to keep the Powers of Europe in union together. And why? Because by keeping all in union together you neutralize and fetter and bind up the selfish aims of each. I am not here to flatter either England or any of them. They have selfish aims, as, unfortunately, we in late years have too sadly shown that we too have had selfish aims; but, then, common action is fatal to selfish aims. Common action means common objects, and the only objects for which you can unite together the Powers of Europe are objects connected with the common good of them all. That, gentlemen, is my third principle of foreign policy.

COLONIAL AND FOREIGN POLICY

'My fourth principle is: That you should avoid needless and entangling engagements. You may boast about them, you may brag about them, you may say you are procuring consideration for the country, you may say that an Englishman can now hold up his head among the nations, you may say that he is not now in the hands of a Liberal Ministry who thought of nothing but pounds, shillings and pence. But what does all this come to? It comes to this, that you are increasing your engagements without increasing your strength; and if you increase engagements without increasing strength, you diminish strength, you abolish strength, you really reduce the Empire, and do not increase it. You render it less capable of performing its duties; you render it an inheritance less precious to hand on to future generations.

'My fifth principle is this: To acknowledge the equal rights of all nations. You may sympathize with one nation more than another—nay, you must sympathize with one nation more than another. You sympathize most with those nations as a rule with which you have the closest connection in language, in blood, and in religion, or whose circumstances at the time seem to give the strongest claim to sympathy. But in point of right all are equal, and you have no right to set up a system under which one of them is to be placed under moral suspicion or espionage, or to be made the constant subject of invective. If you do that, but especially if you claim for yourself a superiority, a pharisaical superiority over the whole of them, then I say you may talk about your patriotism if you please, but you are a misguiding friend of your country, and in undermining the basis of the esteem and respect of other people for your country you are in reality inflicting the severest injury upon it.

'I have now given you five principles of foreign policy. Let me give you a sixth, and then I have done. And that sixth is that in my opinion foreign policy, subject to all the limitations that I have described—the foreign policy of England—should always be inspired by the love of freedom. There should always be a sympathy with freedom, a desire to give it scope, founded not upon visionary ideas, but upon the long experience of many generations within the shores of this happy isle, that in freedom you lay the firmest foundations both of law and order, the firmest foundations for the development of individual character, and the best provision for the happiness of the nation at large. In the foreign policy of this country the name of Canning will ever be honoured, the name of Russell ever will be honoured, the name of Palmerston ever will be honoured by those who recollect the erection of the kingdom of Belgium and the union of the disjointed provinces of Italy. It is that sympathy, not a sympathy with disorder, but, on the contrary,

COLONIAL AND FOREIGN POLICY

founded upon the deepest and most profound love of order—it is that sympathy which in my opinion ought to be the very atmosphere in which a Foreign Secretary of England ought to live and to move.'

The name 'Empire' is charged with associations for which Liberals have little liking, and they would prefer to apply the term 'Commonwealth' to the confederacy of States which makes up the dominions of the Crown. All that has made this Commonwealth great and strong is the work of Liberalism, and Liberalism was never more urgently needed to protect what has been won than in times when men have grown so familiar with its principles as to lose the grasp of their meaning and their value. The wisdom of those principles has been strikingly confirmed by experience.

The Liberal recognises that a wise policy to Ireland will make the honourable nationalism of the Irish people a source of strength instead of a source of danger to the Empire. England and Ireland differ in their religion, their habits, their tastes, their points of strength and weakness, and the problems which they present. To enable Ireland to satisfy and express her aspirations and her character in the opportunities and the forms of Parliamentary institutions is an object of Liberal policy which can only be abandoned with the renunciation of Liberalism itself. And the practical wisdom of allowing such free play to the individuality of national genius

LIBERALISM AND THE EMPIRE

within the Empire as is consistent with the maintenance of Imperial supremacy has been illustrated as often as an Irish political question has presented itself to the attention of Parliament. The necessities of Ireland in land legislation and education are of a nature which the English temperament finds it difficult to understand. At this moment Ireland demands a Catholic University; the English statesmen who have had experience of Irish affairs are agreed that the demand is legitimate, and that something must be done to satisfy it; but the Leader of the House of Commons admits that no Minister could hope to carry through Parliament any measure for settling the problem. Meanwhile, Ireland is suffering all the consequences of the worst form of waste, because English Ministers cannot, or dare not, provide her with the necessary educational machinery. This is only one illustration of the embarrassments created by the present state of affairs. Another might be found in the financial grievances. Unionists argue that the Treaty is alterable or unalterable according as it serves the convenience of a single political party. Ireland is a financial entity for purposes of distribution and not for purposes of taxation. Unionism has not succeeded in solving the material problems of Irish administration, in reconciling Ireland to England, or in extinguishing the spirit of nationalism. And it would indeed be surprising if anything but disaster resulted from a policy which

COLONIAL AND FOREIGN POLICY

has made it the natural thing that an Irish patriot, whether at home or overseas, is regarded and often regards himself as the sworn enemy of the rest of the Empire.

Mr. Gladstone once said that the only striking fact in the history of the relations of the Tory party with the colonies was the loss of the United States. The modern historian must add a second item to that small but disastrous catalogue. When Sir Alfred Milner[1] overruled the wishes of the responsible Governments of Cape Colony and Natal, he deserted the traditions of Liberalism, and he involved South Africa in the worst of all wars—a war of races. It must be the task of Liberals to see that the talk about drawing the Empire more closely together is not to be made a pretext for suffocating the autonomy of our colonies. The attachment of the colonies to Great Britain depends upon conditions which Imperialist Ministers are more likely than anyone or anything else to disturb. A few Milner-Chamberlain combinations are all that is wanted to set the colonies at loggerheads.

And if the future of Ireland and the colonies provides a great task for Liberalism, the duty of impressing upon Englishmen at home their responsibility to India was surely never more imperative. If India

[1] One obviously necessary reform will be the separation of the offices of High Commissioner of South Africa and Governor of Cape Colony.

LIBERALISM AND THE EMPIRE

is to be treated as an end-in-herself, and not merely as a means to the aggrandizement or the enrichment of England, we have little to hope for from the hysterical, unintelligent, bombastic tumult of speech and counsel which calls itself Imperialism. Mr. Gladstone once protested against the iniquity of diverting to frivolous wars the resources which should be husbanded to protect India from the worst horrors of famine. Nearly thirty years later came the Tirah campaign, to be followed by the most terrible of all the famines India has known.

There is an obvious danger that the Empire will be ruled in the interests of our governing families, and it is not difficult to explain why the classes which export younger sons into distant countries as administrators and officials are eager for its expansion. It is the business of Liberalism to secure that public opinion at home shall not be left in ignorance of the conditions of English rule; that India, for example, shall not be secretly deprived of such liberties as she has won; that Englishmen shall not be allowed to regard every Indian famine as an act of God, to be relieved by such charity as they can spare from aggressive enterprises; that private individuals shall not be permitted to disgrace England's flag, to ill-treat her subjects, and to make her the unconscious partner of their crimes. And the hopes of Liberalism at home are bound up with the success of the Liberal attack upon Imperialism. Mr. Hobhouse has shown in a brilliant article[1] that the enemies of Liberalism are the same everywhere. The spirit which has led through the Stock Exchange to foreign adventures, is the same spirit which has led through the power of the vested interests to internal atrophy. Domestic reform, if it is not to be mere empirical legislation wrung from the rich by the threats of the needy, has nothing to hope for until the language of England abroad shall be once again the language of morality, and not 'the language of pride, of mastery, of force, of violence, of revenge'; till England shall honour her old ideals in the larger affairs of humanity; till she shall once more win back the respect instead of drawing upon herself the curses of Liberal Europe; till the love of country and the love of liberty, divorced to-day, shall be brought back into their old glorious association.

[1] *Economic Review*, April, 1899: 'The essence of aristocratic anti-popular sentiment lies in the belief that people of a different class do not bleed when they are pricked, as the aristocrat bleeds; the essence of democratic or popular humanitarian feeling is the belief that whatever differences there are, real or imaginary, between class and class, race and race, they do not override that common human nature which makes elementary justice the same everywhere.' The courageous and consistent opposition to the war maintained by the Labour members is significant and encouraging.

INDEX

A

ABERCORN, Duke of, 51, 54, 60
Aberdeen, Lord, 11, 13
Aborigines Protection Society, 155
Advertisements, Rating of land used for, 93
African Government, 116, 117
Africa, South, Black labour in, 141-145
Agricultural Rates Act, 23, 25
Albu, M., 116
Alsace-Lorraine, 188
America, Slavery in, 138; Domestic service in, 139
Anglo-Saxon, 185, 186
Apportionment, 82
Aristotle on slavery, 133, 134
Armenia, 166
Armenian massacres, 64
Army, Increase of, 107-112
Army League, 110
Asquith, Right Hon. H. H., 85
Athens, 126
Attic law, 127
Australian delegates, 65

B

Baker, Sir James, 146
Balfour, Right Hon. Arthur, 59
Barnato, Barney, 49
Bassermann, Herr, 33
Beaconsfield, Lord, 4, 21, 104; on wise economy, 111, 112, 164, 165, 202
Bechuanaland, 48
Beit, Alfred, 49, 51, 54, 64
Bishops, 172-174
Bismarck, 164
Börsen-politik, 63
Bowles, T. G., 37
Bramwell, Lord, 97
Bright, John, 7, 32; on war, 42, 196, 197
British flag 'a commercial asset,' 58
Brunetière, M., 188
Brussels, Mr., 64
Bryce, Right Hon. James, 142, 143, 175
Budgets, 1895-99, 23-25
Bulawayo, 53
Bullets, Expansive, 146
Bülow, Count von, 32
Burke, Edmund, 3, 26; on the press, 65; on Custom

INDEX

Houses, 69; on Indian Government, 116, 117
Butler, Sir William, attacked, 43
Byron, 166

C

Campbell, Lord, 88
Campbell-Bannerman, Sir Henry, 28, 35, 61, 98, 197
Cannan, Edwin, 81
Canning, 206
Cape Colony, 142
Cardwell, E., and army reform, 22
Carthage, 130
Catholic University in Ireland, 208
Cawston, George, 51, 54
Chamberlain, Right Hon. J., 4, 13; 'long spoon,' etc., 21, 34, 57; on Raid, 61, 179-182, 191-193; relation to Mr. Rhodes, 62; manipulating press, 65-67; on Zollverein, 67-70
Chambers of Commerce, 67-69
Chartered Company, 50; debt, 70, 71
Chartereds, 57
Chatham, 195, 196
Chinese labour, 148; in America and Australia, 137
Churchill, Lord Randolph, 26
Clarendon, Lord, 14
Cobden, Richard, 6-17, 75, 196, 197
Commonwealth, 207
Compound system, 143

Convention between Great Britain and Transvaal, 61, 170
Coolgardie miners, 154
Cornewall Lewis, Sir George, 106
Corvée system, 135
Cotton factories in India, 150
Courtney, Right Hon. Leonard, 93
Crimean War, 111, 112
Cromer, Lord, 73
Curzon, Lord, 22, 194

D

Daily Mail, 135
Daily News, 64, 135, 146, 200-203
Darwin, 171
De Beers, 47-49, 54, 58, 60
De Villiers, Chief Justice, 48
De Worms, Baron, 50
Democracy, Characteristics of, 2
Derby, Lord, 10, 11
Disraeli, Benjamin. See Beaconsfield.
Dreyfus affair, 198
Dum-dum bullet, 6
Dutch finance, 104

E

East Rand, 57
Eckstein, Mr., 49, 64
Economic Journal, 76
Edgeworth, Professor, 85, 86
Egypt, 66, 73, 135
Emporialism, 4, 67
Estimates, Military and naval, 5-41, *passim*

INDEX

Europe, Concert of, 204
Expenditure and Exports, 14-16

F

Farquhar, Sir Horace, 54
Farrer, Lord, on Free Trade, 72, 75
Fashoda, 8, 64, 198
Fatalism, 161 *seq.*
Federation Bill, Australian, 65
Field, Admiral, 34
Fife, Duke of, 51, 54
Fiji, Indenture system in, 136
Financiers, International, 191, 192
Finland, 189
Fitzpatrick, J. P., 56
Flag, Trade and the, 72-74
Food, Taxation of, 109
Fowler, Sir Henry, 56, 203
Fox, 158-160, 165, 197
France, 64, 194; traditional Liberal affection for, 197
Free breakfast-table, 110
Free Trade, 67-70, 109, 110. See Protection.

G

Garrett, Edmund, 64
Germany, 193-195
Gibbon, 46, 47, 151
Gifford, Lord, 51, 54
Gladstone, W. E., 1, 4, 6; as Chancellor of the Exchequer, 15-22; and navy, 26; on war, 42-44; on light wines, 95; on indirect taxes, 106; on economy, 112, 113; his rule, 115; and Imperialism, 199; on international press, 66; principles of foreign policy, 203-207; his nationalism, 165; on Imperium et Libertas, 176, 177; on the equality of nations, 167; on relations of England to Europe, 168, 169
Glen Grey Act, 144
Glenesk, Lord, and Primrose League, 20
Goerz, Herr, 116
Goldfields and gambling, 44, 57
Goschen, Right Hon. G. J., 11, 27-32, 193
Greece, 164; slavery in, 123-129
Grey, Lord, 51, 54, 61, 72, 144
Grootschur, 46
Ground values, Rating of, 83-94

H

Hague Conference, 6, 29
Harcourt, Sir William, 25, 34, 61; on Open Door, 70
Hawksley dossier, 62
Hebrides, New, Frenchmen in, 158
Helot, 128
Herbert, Sidney, 16, 20
Hicks-Beach, Sir Michael, 23; his sale to the Chancellor of the Exchequer, 37; on expenditure, 39, 40; attacked, 43, 59; on

INDEX

Raid, 61; his Budgets of 1899 and 1900, 103, 105, 106; his warning, 110-112
High Commissioner deceived by Mr. Rhodes, 62
Hinterland for supplying slaves, 129
Hobhouse, L. T., 211
Hobson, J. A., on chartered press, 13
Home Rule funds, 50
Horsman, Mr., 20
Huddersfield, 92
Hume, Joseph, 10
Hungary, 164
Huxley, 172

I

Imperialism, growth and species, 3, 4; morality of, 170
Income Tax, Graduation of, 113
Indenture system, 136
India, 209
Indwe coal-mine, 48
Inebriates, 99
International financiers, 191, 192
Investors' Review, 48
Ireland, 207-209
Issues 'to meet other expenditure,' 35, 36
Italian immigration into America, 139
Italy, 164

J

Jameson Raid, 53, 59, 71, 179, 181

K

Kanakas, 134, 136, 153
Kekewich, Colonel, 58
Kenhardt, 64
Khaki loan, 103
Kiao-Chou, 194
Kimberley, 47; servitude and population, 49, 143
Kipling, Rudyard, 188
Kossuth, 164
Kruger, President, 57

L

Labouchere, H., 54
Labour, Compulsory, 56
Lambton, Captain Hedworth, 199
Lansdowne, Lord, his 'normal increase,' 37
Lascars, 138
Lauder, Captain, 146
Lawson, Sir Wilfrid, 66
Lecky, W. E. H., 55
License duties, Table of, 101
Licenses, 52, 96-101
Liquor laws, 95-101
Lo Bengula, 52
Location system, 143
Long Tom, 44
Louis Philippe, 9
Lyndhurst, Lord, 20

M

Machiavelli, 67
Madden, Sir J., 65
Magdalen College, Oxford, 47
Magersfontein, 58
Maguire, Rochfort, 54

INDEX

Majuba, 200
Marshall, Professor, 85
Mashonaland, 52, 53
Matabele, 134, 183
Matabele War, 59
Matabeleland, 52, 53
Mazzini, 164
Meredith, Mr. George, 197
Metternich, 164
Militia Act of 1852, 10
Milner, Sir Alfred, 13, 128, 209
Modder River, 58
Modders, 57
Monopoly, Gibbon on, 46, 47; of De Beers, 47-49; of Chartered Company, 49-52; local and natural, 91, 92; liquor, 98-101
Morley, Right Hon. J., 33, 181, 195, 197
Morning Leader, 53
Mungo Park, 140

N

Napoleon Bonaparte, 162
Napoleon, Louis, English attacks on, 10, 13
Natal, 142
National Debt, Moral value of, 103
National Liberal Federation, 63
Nationalism, 165-167, 188, 189, 192
Navy, British, 5-35, *passim*
Navy, French, 5
Navy, German, 32, 33
Navy League, 34, 110
New South Wales, 154
Nicias, 128

Nigger, 121
Nottingham, 63

O

Oriel College, 47

P

Pacifico, Don, 166
Palmerston, Lord, 4, 8, 10, 16, 20, 21, 65, 112, 166
Panic, The fourth, 26
Panics, The Three, 7-13; God of, 21
Parnell, Charles Stewart, 50
Patronage of Justices, 97
Payment of election expenses and of members, 114
Peel, Lord, his minority report, 98
Peel, Sir Robert, 1, 5-7, 33, 106, 197
Perks, R. W., 20
Peters, Dr., 153
Pitt, 5
Poland, Sir Harry, 87-90
Port Arthur, 195
Press, Chamberlainite, 42, 67; international, 66
Press, Monopoly of, 12, 13; power of, 64; remedy for, 114
Press, Rhodesian, 42
Press, Yellow, 10
Privy Council, 45, 46
Privy Councillor, his oath, 60
Protection, Revival of, 105-110. See Free Trade.

INDEX

Q

Queensland, Forced labour in, 134-137, 143, 153, 154

R

Racial differences in British Empire, 120
Ralph, Julian, 58
Ramsden, Sir John, 92
Rand mines, 57
Rates, 70-94
Red Indians, 49
Reid, Sir Robert, 61, 62
Rhodes, Right Hon. Cecil, 13; his honour, classics, lions, etc., 46; De Beers, 47-49; acquires charter, 49-52; his profits, 52-54; his Raid, 55, 59-62; on the war, 57-62, 64; on Rhodesian tariff, 70, 71; on flags, 192
Rhodesia, 50
Rhodesia Herald, 52, 53
Roberts, Lord, 146
Rome, Slavery in, 129-131, 149
Rothschild, Lord, 54
Rowntree, Joseph, 101
Rudd, 54
Russell, Lord John, 10; on licenses, 99
Russia, 189, 194, 195

S

Salisbury, Lord, 20, 22, 42, 43, 73, 115, 195
Salisbury Plain, 37
Scully, 145
Sepoys, 145
Service Committees, 35

Shaw-Lefevre, Right Hon. G., 27
Sherwell, A., 97
Slatin, Sir Rudolf, 135
Slav, 121
Slave, Definition of, 121, 149
Slavery, Economic effects of, 131
Smith, Adam, 32; on monopoly, 49, 50, 84-87
Smith, Orford, 87-90
Somerset, Duke of, 16
Soudan, 73, 135
Speaker, 76
Spencer, Herbert, 172, 174, 180
Spencer, Lord, 27
Stead, W. T., and panic of 1883, 26
Sub-Editor, Power of, 63
Sugar, Duty on, 108
Sunday Observer, 30, 31
Syrian dispute, 8
Syrophœnicia, 4; colonists from, 4

T

Tasmanians, 149
The Times newspaper, 13, 35, 37, 63-65, 103
Thomson, H. C., 48
Times expert, 104-109
Tithes, 25
Toronto, 68
Transvaal Republic, 6, 166, 189
Treasury control, Attack on, 42, 43

U

Uganda railway, 74
Uitlander agitation, Hollowness of, 43

INDEX

V
Van Wyk's Vlei, 63
Voltaire, 163, 172
Voluntary schools, 25

W
Walpole, 195, 196
Walpole, Sir Spencer, 197
Walton, Miss, 63, 64
War, Crimean, 43
War, Finance of, 41-45
War, South African, Cost of, 40, 41; financial, 44, 45

Warner, Courtenay, 38
'Wealth of Nations,' 85
Wellington, Duke of, 8
Wemyss, Lord, 20
Wesselton mine, 48
Westminster Gazette, 146

Y
Young, Arthur, 106

Z
Zambesi, 48
Zollverein, 67-69

THE END

BOOKS PUBLISHED BY R. BRIMLEY JOHNSON

All net Prices

LIBERALISM AND THE EMPIRE

by

FRANCIS W. HIRST GILBERT MURRAY

and

J. L. HAMMOND

Crown 8vo. Three shillings and sixpence net.

READY

TWO STAGE PLAYS

DENZILL HERBERT'S ATONEMENT : BONDAGE

by

LUCY SNOWE

Royal 16*mo. Three shillings net.*

DENZILL HERBERT'S ATONEMENT and BONDAGE are domestic dramas of modern life, serious studies in normal character. Although—as expressly implied by the title—they are written for, and adapted to, stage performance, they possess the sustained human interest of all vital fiction (narrative or dramatic), and should prove a welcome addition to the Library of Modern Dramatists which the ardent reader has lately been enabled to form. We are just beginning to recognise that plays which are worthy of serious attention should be read as well as seen, and that the English drama may once more become a living force.

FORTHCOMING

OTHER VOLUMES
BY LUCY SNOWE

THE PAYING GUEST
a Comedy.

SUBURBIA
Stories,
Etc.

READY

[Transferred to R. Brimley Johnson.]

LAMBKIN'S REMAINS

by

H. B.

Author of *The Bad Child's Book of Beasts, The Modern Traveller, More Beasts for Worse Children,* etc.

'Highly diverting.'—*Morning Post.*
'Delightful fooling.'—*Academy.*
'A feast of humour.'—*Review of the Week.*
'An irresistible study in mediocrity.'—*Black and White.*
'A humorous creation of the first rank ... Amazingly clever.'—*The Star.*

Two shillings net.

8, York Buildings, Adelphi,
London, W.C.

CPSIA information can be obtained at www.ICGtesting.com
265615BV00007B/26/P